CREATING MAGIC

CREATING MAGIC

10 Common Sense Leadership Strategies from

a Life at Disney

LEE COCKERELL

DOUBLEDAY

NEW YORK LONDON TORONTO SYDNEY AUCKLAND

DOUBLEDAY

Copyright © 2008 by Lee Cockerell

All Rights Reserved

Published in the United States by Doubleday, an imprint of The Doubleday Publishing
Group, a division of Random House, Inc., New York.
www.doubleday.com

DOUBLEDAY is a registered trademark and the DD colophon is a trademark
of Random House, Inc.

All trademarks are the property of their respective companies.

Book design by Diane Hobbing of Snap-Haus Graphics

Library of Congress Cataloging-in-Publication Data
Cockerell, Lee.
Creating magic : 10 common sense leadership strategies from a life at Disney / by Lee
Cockerell.
p.   cm.
Includes index.
1. Leadership. 2. Corporate culture. 3. Organizational effectiveness. 4. Walt Disney
World (Fla.) 5. Walt Disney Company—Management. I. Title.
HD57.7.C62 2008
658.4'092—dc22
2008003338

ISBN 978-0-385-52386-8

PRINTED IN THE UNITED STATES OF AMERICA

13 15 17 19 20 18 16 14 12

FOR
Jullian Charles Cockerell, 13
Margot Sunshine Cockerell, 10
Tristan Lee Cockerell, 7
You are the leaders of tomorrow.
You continually inspire me
to be a better leader and role model.
I love you—Papi

CONTENTS

Foreword by Frances Hesselbein   ix

Acknowledgments   xiii

Chapter One   MAKING MAGIC   1

Chapter Two   THE JOURNEY FROM THE FARM TO A
                     MAGIC KINGDOM   17

Chapter Three   STRATEGY #1
                     REMEMBER, EVERYONE IS IMPORTANT   32

Chapter Four   STRATEGY #2
                     BREAK THE MOLD   56

Chapter Five   STRATEGY #3
                     MAKE YOUR PEOPLE YOUR BRAND   85

Chapter Six   STRATEGY #4
                     CREATE MAGIC THROUGH TRAINING   114

Chapter Seven   STRATEGY #5
                     ELIMINATE HASSLES   143

Chapter Eight   STRATEGY #6
                     LEARN THE TRUTH   168

Chapter Nine   STRATEGY #7
                     BURN THE FREE FUEL   187

Chapter Ten   STRATEGY #8
                     STAY AHEAD OF THE PACK   208

Chapter Eleven   STRATEGY #9
                     BE CAREFUL WHAT YOU SAY AND DO   230

Chapter Twelve   STRATEGY #10
                     DEVELOP CHARACTER   247

Chapter Thirteen   LEADING INTO THE FUTURE   260

Appendix   DISNEY INSTITUTE   264

Index   266

C reating Magic, Lee Cockerell's new book, does just that! As the Executive Vice President of Operations for the Walt Disney World® Resort, for ten years Lee led a team of 40,000 cast members whose daily challenge was to create magic for the millions of people who visited the parks and resorts. With this book, Lee takes us on a leadership adventure—not just in theory, but an actual real-life journey along which you will learn how to build a passionate team whose members believe: "It's not the magic that makes it work; it's the way we work that makes it magic." Creating Magic is not about the theory of magic, but the live, on-the-ground experience of an icon in the magic business—Lee Cockerell.

This remarkable story of a leadership journey is filled with common sense lessons about making magic that we can translate into our own careers, business cultures, or visions of the desired future. Lee shows how, at Disney, leadership starts with respect for all people—Guests and Cast Members (not "employees") alike. Lee's approach helps us remember Peter Drucker and his philosophy: "They are not your employees, they are your people." Lee has distilled his lessons learned into short, powerful messages that connect, illuminate, and motivate.

The Disney Great Leader Strategies that Lee developed are the basis for this handbook for leaders of the future. As Lee's story shows, fostering participation, engagement, and a sense of ownership at every level across the Disney world brought high morale, high productivity, and real results. Lee's story is about moving from the old hierarchy to an inclusive, flexible, fluid, inclusive structure—from "telling" to "asking." These missions, values, and strategies have made Disney a great learning organization, and at the Disney Institute, they have helped bring people from all over the world together to learn to be better leaders.

Lee Cockerell's journey began on a dusty Oklahoma farm, and the lessons he learned along the way—from the farm, to college, to the United States Army, and in the hospitality and entertainment industries—provided the lessons indispensable to the future leader he would become.

He learned the power of inclusion that later became "RAVE": respect, appreciate, and value everyone. His thirteen steps to creating a culture of inclusion give clear and powerful direction. All the way through the book, you will learn the value of people—and how to redefine the future by infusing quality, character, truth, communication, learning, courage, and integrity in all you do.

Even in his acknowledgments, Lee thanks all the Cast Members at Disney World "for all you've taught me over the years. You are the magic." Lee's leadership is never about him, but always about the people. Leading into an uncertain future, there is a call for principled, ethical, effective leaders—not repeating the strategies and philosophies of the past, but redefining the future—the opportunities, the challenges, the ambiguities. Lee Cockerell's lessons from his own life provide a road map, a handbook, for us all on our journey to leadership. The leaders of tomorrow, called to lead in uncertain times, will translate *Creating Magic* into their own guidebook for the future.

The lessons in this book apply to leaders at every level in every type of organization and in every country on this earth. Lee's common sense leadership strategies can help all people understand that leadership is not a title or a position, it is a personal responsibility.

I guarantee you that this book will help you create magic in your business life, your community life, and your personal life.

Today, Lee travels, speaks, writes, engages, and shares as generously in person as he does in this great book.

Frances Hesselbein
Chairman and Founding President
Leader to Leader Institute

Frances Hesselbein is the Chairman of the Board of Governors of the Leader to Leader Institute (formerly the Peter F. Drucker Foundation for Nonprofit Management) and served as its Founding President. She was awarded the Presidential Medal of Freedom, the United States of America's highest civilian honor, in 1998. The award recognized her leadership as Chief Executive Officer of Girl Scouts of the U.S.A. from 1976 to 1990, and her role as the founding President of the Drucker Foundation. President Clinton, in his opening citation, said, "Mrs. Hesselbein is a pioneer for women, diversity, and inclusion." Her contributions were also recognized by former president George H. W. Bush, who appointed her to two Presidential Commissions on National and Community Service.

ACKNOWLEDGMENTS

I am grateful and indebted to the following people for their contributions to this book and to my life. Everyone matters, and I want everyone to know he or she matters.

First and foremost, to my wife, Priscilla: You taught me the ultimate leadership lesson when you told me so many years ago, "Lee, be careful what you say and do, they are watching you and judging you." Thank you for that, for your unwavering faith and support, and for forty wonderful years together through thick and thin.

To the rest of my family: our son, Daniel, and his wife, Valerie, who are both great leaders at home and at work; our perfect grandchildren, Jullian, Margot, and Tristan, who teach me valuable lessons every day; my mother-in-law, Sunshine Payne, whose first name describes what she brings to our lives; and all my extended family members, near and far—the Cockerells, the Paynes, the Kenagas, the Cooks, the Howards, and the Vettards.

To Philip Goldberg: Thank you for taking the original manuscript I wrote, plus everything else I have written over the years, plus my thoughts and concepts on leadership, and then taking this book to a new level. You and I went from acquaintances to friends as we wrote this book together. (Phil in turn wants to thank his wife, Lori Deutsch, for encouraging him to take on this project and for supporting it enthusiastically throughout.)

To my agent, Lynn Franklin: Thank you for forty years of friendship; for urging me to write this book, for bringing Phil Goldberg and me together, and for your professional expertise in getting the book published around the world.

To my New York attorney, Stephen Sheppard: Thank you for keeping me out of trouble and getting all of those contracts straight.

To my Disney partners: Bob Gall, for your guidance, and for keeping us all on track and moving forward; George Aguel, for your support for having this book written; Thomas Katheder, for your great legal reviews, your advice, and your excellent editing and content recommendations; Chris Ambrose, Amy Groff, Bruce Jones, Sara Jones, Cynthia Michalos-Baker, Ken Miratsky, Rob Morton, Tom Nabbe, Jeff Noel, Joanne Recek, Mary Ellen Starnes, Beth Stevens, and Chris Szydlo, for your advice and direction on content and marketing.

To all the Cast Members at *Walt Disney World*® Resort: Thank you for all you've taught me over the years. You are the magic!

To the Disney Institute clients from various companies who contributed their stories or helped me gather stories from others: Jeff Adler, Bruce Cummings, Johan De Beer, Melanie French, John Kelly, Marylynne Kelts, Laurie Kotas, Stuart McDonald, Anton Potgieter, Jim Purvis, Frank Richards, and Bill Valk. Thank you all for your enthusiasm and generosity.

To Chris Moore, a good friend and former colleague, for your historical briefing on the birth of the leadership and cultural changes that Judson Green gave birth to at Walt Disney World.

To Trish Hunt, a good friend, former colleague, and my current vice president of marketing, for your insights and stories on how effective Disney Great Leader Strategies have been in your career.

To the Doubleday team: Roger Scholl, for recognizing the promise of the book, and for your enthusiasm and encouragement throughout; Talia Krohn, for your candid, professional feedback and excellent editing (Phil and I loved working with you); Meredith McGinnis and Jillian Wohlfarth, for your excellent marketing plan; and Elizabeth Hazelton, for your work on publicity.

CHAPTER ONE

MAKING MAGIC

I t's not the magic that makes it work; it's the way we work that makes it magic." Everyone who works at *Walt Disney World*® Resort learns that principle, and the result has been magic for the Guests and for the bottom line. Now you can create magic too—for your organization, your family, and your community—by following the leadership strategies in this book.

During my sixteen years as a senior Disney executive, I repeated that phrase about making magic hundreds of times. But its full magnitude hit me with hurricane force—literally—in the summer of 2004. That's when Disney World was hammered by three major hurricanes in a little more than a month. Normally, tropical storms do not cause heavy damage in Orlando, as it is about fifty miles from both coasts. In fact, the city had not suffered a direct hit in forty-four years. Then came 2004 and the one-two punch of Charley and Frances.

In August, Hurricane Charley swept through Orlando on Friday the thirteenth with gusts of up to 105 miles per hour, ripping down trees and power lines and tearing the roofs off buildings. The area had not yet fully recovered when Frances came roaring in two weeks later—on Labor Day weekend, no less, when Disney World was host to seventy-five thousand guests. We were forced to close the theme parks on both occasions, something we had done only twice before, once on 9/11 and once in 1999 for Hurricane Floyd, which fortunately veered away at the last minute. But this time we had to batten down the hatches, and when your hatches are spread over forty-seven square miles, it's a monumental task.

What I remember most about the ordeal is not the terrifying winds or the sleepless nights in the emergency operation center (EOC), where my team and I had gathered to make plans to ensure the safety of our Guests and fellow Cast Members.* Instead, I remember the dedication of our staff, the precision of our communications, and the smooth way everyone did what he or she was supposed to do even though it'd never been done before. I remember teams of dedicated people tying down chandeliers, stacking tables and chairs and roping them together, and strapping vending carts to the ground. I remember Mickey and Minnie and Cinderella and Goofy cheering up frightened children in the hotel lobbies. Mostly, I remember the five-thousand-plus Cast Members who spent the stormy nights on the property so they could help at any hour and in any way they could, and the countless others who showed up with their sleeves rolled up the minute it was safe to leave their homes.

I also remember this: When Charley finally subsided, around midnight, exhausted Cast Members worked through the night, clearing debris, getting supplies to where they were needed, and hauling away thousands of damaged trees. It was a monumental effort, with everyone acting as one to get the parks

---

*Walt Disney World capitalizes words such as "Cast Member" (the term used for employees) and "Guest" as a reminder to everyone how critically important they are. I will follow that convention in this book.

ready for our Guests, some of whom had been stuck in their rooms for eighteen hours. The next morning, we opened on time. And the families who poured in were astonished to find the sunlit theme parks looking spotless and the operations running as if nothing had happened. What they could not see was the massive teamwork behind the scenes that made it all possible or the stress and fatigue behind the smiling faces that greeted them. While many other attractions and businesses in central Florida remained closed and local municipalities were struggling to restore power and clear the roads, Disney was making magic.

As the executive vice president in charge of operations at Disney World, I could not have been more proud. All the work that my colleagues and I had done to instill strong leadership values throughout the company had clearly paid off. We already knew that our basic principles worked, but it's easy to think you're doing well when times are good. The real test comes when a crisis hits, and our response to this one validated everything I had learned and tried diligently to teach others. Thanks to the solid structures and processes we had in place, everyone knew exactly where to go and what to do. More important, each Cast Member was prepared, mentally and emotionally, to let the vision of Disney World govern everything he or she did: treat the Guests as cherished friends, exceed their expectations, and give them the best vacation experience of their lives. Everyone from top executives to rookies pursued this vision with remarkable dedication.

Soon I would be even more proud. Our company immediately set out to help Cast Members and area residents who had suffered major losses because of the hurricanes. Cast Members at every level of pay came through, either with direct donations or by converting their accrued vacation time into cash. With those funds and the millions more contributed directly by the Walt Disney Company, we were able to provide substantial financial aid, along with supplies, lodging, child care, and other services, to those in need.

All in all, what we saw in that tumultuous period is the kind of strong commitment and exceptional performance that any organization can enjoy as long as its leaders treat people with respect and unite them all behind one common purpose. When things returned to normal and I read the hundreds of letters we'd received from grateful Guests, I made a personal decision: The minute I retired, I would write a book about Disney's leadership strategies, so that people in every industry and every walk of life could learn how to create the same kind of magic in their organizations and in their lives. This is that book, and I'm certain that no matter what position you now hold—whether you've just started your very first job or you're the CEO of a multinational corporation—you will be a better leader if you follow the ten common sense strategies that follow.

THE WORLD OF DISNEY WORLD

The enchanted realm called Walt Disney World is about the size of San Francisco, or *twice* the size of Manhattan. As the largest tourist destination and one of the biggest convention sites in the world, its 25,000 acres include 32 hotels with more than 31,000 rooms, hundreds of dining and retail locations, four major theme parks, a sports and recreation complex, a shopping and entertainment village, and 167 miles of roadway. With its 59,000 Cast Members, it is the largest single-site employer in the world. And my job was to know exactly what was going on in every nook and cranny of that vast domain.

For ten years I was responsible for making sure everything from the removal of trash to the operation of rides and attractions ran as smoothly and impeccably as a Swiss watch. In order to do my job, I had to know what our Guests felt about their time with us, and so I read their letters over the years, thousands of them, and I can say beyond a shadow of a doubt that it's not just the great weather, fabulous shows, and thrilling attractions that bring millions of people a year to Disney World. Those all are extremely important, of course, but what *really* drives the magic is the extraordinary service. How does Disney maintain that high-quality service? Each of the fifty-nine thousand Cast Members is trained to treat each and every Guest with the utmost care and respect. And they do this consistently because they are treated exactly the same way by the Disney leadership: with the utmost care and respect.

If that sounds like a commercial for a fluffy feel-good Disney movie, let me assure you it's not. It's a rational, muscular, no-nonsense business strategy. And its results are reflected in Disney's robust bottom line, not to mention its astonishing 70 percent return rate among visitors and the lowest employee turnover rate of any major company in the hospitality industry. The formula is simple: Committed, responsible, inspiring leaders create a culture of care, which leads to quality service, which leads to Guest satisfaction, which leads to measurable business results and a strong competitive advantage.

Products and services can easily be replicated. So if your company's competitive advantage is based on products and services alone, you are at risk. But if it's based upon products, services, and *quality service*, then you'll have a competitive advantage that's very difficult to match. And you can get quality service only by creating a caring, respectful, people-centered culture within your company. Take care of your people, and they will take care of your business, not just because they *have* to but because they *want* to.

KEEPING UP WITH CHANGE

Walt Disney himself created the template for quality service when he first envisioned theme parks more than half a century ago. Later, in 1982, the company's reputation got a powerful boost when Tom Peters praised it in his mega-selling book *In Search of Excellence*. Because Peters singled out the Disney training procedures, managers and executives from other companies started asking how they could emulate those methods.

Throughout the 1980s, Disney World continued to thrive financially. But by the early 1990s, the times were a-changin'. Competitors were starting to catch up, and certain aspects of the company's management style began to seem outdated. The autocratic, top-down leadership approach of the past was less and less welcome in the changing social landscape; management experts predicted that the coming generation of workers and managers would thrive better in a more democratic, participatory environment. One visionary leader who saw the writing on the wall was Judson Green, who was then the president of Disney's Theme Parks and Resorts division. If Walt Disney World was going to adapt to an evolving society and maintain its industry dominance, he realized, the corporate culture had to change.

Intuitively, Judson knew that the key to continued financial success was to provide Guests with a wonderful experience so they'd come back again and again and recommend the place to their families and friends. He reasoned that the Guests' satisfaction depended on the quality of service they received. After all, studies in a variety of industries have shown that it's not just the product that makes for satisfied customers; it's the way they are treated. Judson also knew what I too had learned over the course of my career: If you want your employees to deliver excellent service, you'd better provide them with excellent leadership. A few years later we tested this theory analytically, by conducting a research study. The results showed clearly that Guests were far more likely to return if they were satisfied with their previous visit, and their satisfaction level was highest when they had positive interactions with Cast Members. What was the key to producing that? Effective leadership. The study found that business units with the highest scores in Guest satisfaction were the same ones whose leaders received high ratings from their direct reports in qualities such as listening, coaching, recognizing people's efforts, and giving people decision-making authority. In short, great leadership leads to employee excellence, which leads to customer satisfaction and strong business results. In other words, the customer doesn't come first; *leadership* comes first.

THE DISNEY FORMULA FOR SUCCESS
· ·

Leadership ▷ Cast (Employee) Excellence ▷ Guest (Customer)
Satisfaction ▷ Business Results

So Judson Green and Al Weiss, the new executive vice president, set out to implement that formula by revamping the management style at Walt Disney World. That's where I came in.

In May 1993, I was vice president of resort operations at Euro Disney (now Disneyland Paris). My wife, Priscilla, and I were living in France, preparing for our son Daniel's wedding to our wonderful daughter-in-law, Valerie, when I was offered the post of senior vice president of resort operations at Walt Disney World, reporting directly to Al Weiss. I'm sure there were many reasons for that promotion, and one of them was surely my passion for leadership excellence. Judson, with whom I'd worked in Paris, knew that I had been studying the subject for many years and had implemented key leadership principles during my time with the company, as well as earlier, when I had worked for Marriott.

So Priscilla and I picked up and moved to Florida. Pretty soon I was playing a key role in transforming the corporate culture at the world's most successful resort. The mandate was clear: In an era of rapid change, our management style had to be as creative as the movies produced by Disney's animators and as innovative as the attractions dreamed up by Disney's Imagineers (creative designers). We needed leaders who could both manage the business and inspire our Cast Members to adapt to twenty-first-century demands.

A TIME OF TRANSITION

Disney was already renowned for its excellent training procedures at the time, but that training did not include leadership. This was about to change. Now we would make it our policy to promote leadership excellence among our Cast and follow through with clear expectations and ongoing education. And that meant *everyone*. The idea was to achieve leadership excellence by spreading responsibility and authority throughout the organization. We understood that anyone at any level—from the landscape and cleaning crews right on up to the CEO of the whole organization—can exert leadership and make a positive difference. We let it be known that managers and executives would be evaluated not only on their bottom line results but on *how* those results were obtained. Everyone was now expected to live up to specific values and ideals. "My way or the highway" would be replaced by "What do you think?" as leaders were expected to encourage ongoing input and to show Cast Members that their ideas were valued and their needs were taken seriously.

The road to performance excellence was bumpy at first; change always meets with resistance, and this was no exception. Some of the old guard were set in their ways and were unwilling or unable to get on board. We heard many variations of "It ain't broke, so why fix it?" and we lost some competent managers along the way; some of our leaders left the company in the first eighteen months. But eventually the new direction paid off big-time.

Most leaders saw merit in what we were doing and learned to adapt, even though it wasn't easy at times. One prime example was Tom Nabbe. Tom had started working for Disneyland in Anaheim when he was in junior high, just after the park opened. Red-haired and freckled, he was the very first "Tom Sawyer" on Tom Sawyer's Island. He later moved into supervisory roles and relocated to Orlando in 1971. Eventually he became the manager of distribution services for warehousing. After more than thirty years at Disney, Tom was used to the old management style, in which the people in charge handed down directions and the staff were expected to execute them exactly as they were told. Now, like all the other managers, Tom was asked to step back, loosen the reins, and inspire his team to develop its own procedures and discover its own solutions. "It was a time of introspection for me," he recalls. "I was a little skeptical at first, but the philosophy behind the Performance Excellence campaign started to make sense. I learned how to develop real teamwork, where everything we did supported what we called the three-legged stool: the Guests, the Cast Members, and the business metrics. I became a better leader, and everything got done better, faster, and cheaper."

Tom, who retired in 2003 after forty-seven years with the company, remembers the time that the process of handling materials was brought up-to-date with new technology. Under the old management style, automating a major operation would have been met with strong resistance from disgruntled workers. Instead, the frontline staff met the challenge head-on. Because they were involved from conception to execution, not only did they feel a sense of ownership in the new system, but their ideas proved to be invaluable. As a result, products got from the warehouse to the end users a lot faster, and Tom's team received accolades from trade magazines and industry experts.

Once the changes were firmly in place, we quickly saw concrete evidence of the results, which convinced Tom and other managers that we were headed in the right direction. The average score on our annual leadership survey went up, and the average continued to rise annually at a rate that business analysts called incredible.

THE GREAT LEADER STRATEGIES

Two years later, in 1995, I realized that the new leadership philosophy was not being implemented as quickly and as universally as we had hoped it would. So I decided to make the basic concepts more concrete. Drawing on everything I had learned over thirty-five years in the hospitality industry, and with the help of a friend and management consultant named Jamie Conglose, I wrote them out in a clear, simple, and easy-to-follow form. The result was what came to be called the Disney Great Leader Strategies, which soon became the bedrock principles by which the company's seven thousand leaders operate. And it's these same strategies that now provide the foundation for this book.

Once the strategies took hold, bottom line results quickly followed: The percentage of returning Guests steadily increased; scores on leadership evaluations improved dramatically each year; employee turnover dropped to its present level, the lowest in the hospitality industry and a third of the industry average. The rollout of the strategies took only eight weeks. I began by going over each strategy and tactic with my direct reports. Then they spent two weeks reviewing them in detail with their own direct reports. This chain continued until the strategies had been reviewed by every single manager. We then made copies available to all the Cast Members so they would know what leadership behaviors to expect from their managers. Because the strategies were taught to all Cast Members (they were even recorded on CDs, which Cast Members could borrow or buy), everyone, from stage hands to supervisors to upper management, became fully committed to one common purpose: making sure that every Guest had the most fantastic time of his or her life.

Without these strong values and the solid leadership training to implement them, Walt Disney World might not have made it through the tumultuous nineties with the remarkable reputation and competitive edge it still enjoys today.

I assure you the strategies don't apply just to theme parks and resorts, and they don't work just for world-famous brands like Disney. They are effective at every level of every industry, in any location, whether a corner shop or a retail conglomerate; a hospital or a bowling alley; Wall Street or Silicon Valley; a London bank or a German automobile plant; a Japanese electronics firm or a Bangalore call center. And they work not only in the corporate world but also in the nonprofit sector, in everything from schools to religious organizations, as well as in community life, the military, and even parenting! After all, Disney is just like every business, including yours, whatever it may be: It has to make a profit, it has to deal with serious business issues, it faces intense competition, and its strongest competitor is its own reputation.

Over the course of many years and hundreds of seminars and lectures, I've taught the same principles to leaders from every continent and a vast array of cultures, and I've never found anyone anywhere who does not recognize their validity. In short, the strategies in this book can benefit anyone who wants to make a difference and leave a legacy of positive leadership.

My former colleague Trish Hunt is a good example of someone who used the Great Leader Strategies (GLS) as a road map to success in a number of different arenas. She first learned the principles you're about to learn when she worked in human resources at Walt Disney World. She later applied them in executive positions at Cooperstown Dreams Park as well as two large financial institutions. "If I didn't have the Great Leader Strategies to reference, I wouldn't have had the success I did," she told me. "Applying what I learned about leadership, following the different steps, and sharing ideas from the strategies opened doors for me with other executives and with my staff. It translated to high performance and productivity. In the three years I was at one bank, none of my direct reports was terminated or resigned, customer satisfaction increased steadily, and I reduced my budget several million dollars by applying specific tools from the GLS." Throughout the book you'll hear from other leaders who have successfully applied the strategies in their organizations.

THE DISNEY INSTITUTE

When you do something really well, the word tends to get out. Soon more and more businesses were asking to learn about Disney's training methods, so a full-fledged professional development institute was established. Today the Disney Institute (DI) attracts more than a hundred thousand people a year to its open enrollment courses and specially tailored programs. People from all kinds of companies around the globe come to improve their leadership skills, business practices, work environment, and customer service.

The DI draws clients from a wide range of industries—from health care to financial services to manufacturing—and from virtually every country with a modern economy. At a recent seminar, for example, there were people from a South African mining company, a large Canadian restaurant chain, a park district in the California desert, a small Pennsylvania college, an international investment banking firm, a foster care agency, a small auto dealership in Mississippi, a large health maintenance organization, the Rock and Roll Hall of Fame and Museum, Hewlett-Packard, and the National Security Agency. In fact, as I was editing this book, the *Washington Post* reported that 2,000 employees of Walter Reed Army Medical Center would be required to take a Disney Institute training program. The hospital is implementing a command-wide culture change to ensure that everyone who enters its doors leaves having had a positive experience. The quality of medical care provided for patients was never in question. But inadequate housing facilities and frustrating bureaucratic processes for disability evaluation led to well-publicized complaints from patients and family members. The hospital turned to Disney for help in changing its culture. Colonel Patricia D. Horoho, commander of Walter Reed's health-care system, explained why: "When you enter the hospital, we want it to be the best experience possible."

Seeing how effective the Great Leader Strategies were in practice, the DI began to incorporate them into its training programs. The strategies now form the basis of the institute's core curriculum, providing the foundation for courses such as Leadership Excellence, Quality Service, and Organizational Creativity. In essence, the Disney Institute uses both classroom instruction and real-life demonstrations in the actual Disney operation to teach companies of all types how to make the Disney approach work in their business or industry. Their courses take people from the principle to the practice so quickly and seamlessly that once the training is over, attendees can immediately begin to implement them to become better leaders in their own organizations. (See Appendix for more information about the institute.)

The point is that every person in these training programs leaves better equipped to lead his or her organization to better results. Why? Because all business problems boil down to leadership problems. Everything you wish to accomplish is driven by great leadership, and the strategies for achieving that are the same regardless of the industry you're in, the continent you're on, the products or services you provide, or the number of workers you employ.

The ideas in the coming chapters are as simple as they are profound. They sound like good old-fashioned common sense, and they *are* common sense. But unfortunately they are *not* common practice. I've known a lot of powerful, highly competent executives in my time. Most of them can describe their business strategies in great detail yet have very little to say about their leadership strategies. And many of those who can talk the talk don't necessarily walk it. They train people to manage just fine, but they fail to appreciate the critical difference between managing and leading. I learned the hard way that managerial skills are absolutely essential for getting results, but they are not enough to drive *excellence*. Excellence requires common sense leadership.

One of the great misconceptions about leadership is that it's an innate gift that can't be taught. People assume that leaders are born, not made. Another misconception is that leadership is synonymous with titles, job descriptions, and salary grades. It's not. Leadership is more than a role; it's a responsibility. A big one. Being a leader means doing what has to be done, when it has to be done, in the way it *should* be done, whether you like it or not, and whether *they* like it or not. It means making the right things happen by bringing out the best in others. I like to say that good leaders are environmentalists. Their responsibility is to create a sustainable business environment—calm, clear, crisp, and clean, with no pollution, no toxins, no waste— in which everyone flourishes.

Everyone can exert that kind of leadership. The top-to-bottom principles in this book can be taught to people at every level of any enterprise, and the results are predictable: increased trust, motivation, and teamwork, plus an emotional connection that resonates throughout the organization, spreading from one employee to another and then outward to the hearts and minds of customers.

That's what makes the difference between ordinary performance and magic. I have repeatedly seen the strategies in this book transform managers into leaders, poor leaders into good leaders, and good leaders into great leaders who create the kind of environment that everyone dreams of working in and that customers return to again and again.

The purpose of this book is to offer leaders and potential leaders the same powerful strategies that have worked magic at Disney World and for the clients of the Disney Institute. Two of the ten strategies emphasize the nuts and bolts of organizational structure and business procedures. The others focus on dealing with people. That 80:20 ratio reflects the vital importance of inspiring, motivating, teaching, and other so-called soft skills. As I tell every audience I address, the soft stuff is actually the hard stuff, but if you get it right, everything else tends to fall into place and turns out to be not so hard after all.

I've often wished that someone had taught me these leadership truths early in my career. (Actually my mother and grandmother did teach them to me, but I forgot them when I got into the corporate world.) Had I remembered them, I would have been spared a great many costly mistakes. Then again, I learned from those mistakes, and I take great pleasure in knowing that this book will help other leaders avoid the same pitfalls. But before we get into the leadership strategies themselves, let me fill you in on how my own life and career led me to them.

CHAPTER TWO

THE JOURNEY FROM THE FARM
TO A MAGIC KINGDOM

I f my high school classmates and teachers knew about my career, they'd most likely be shaking their heads in surprise. They probably figured I'd end up running a local supply shop, not a multibillion-dollar enterprise with fifty-nine thousand employees. Frankly, I'm astonished myself. I never had a career plan. I had no five-year goals. I just did the best work I could. I worked hard and tried to be responsible, patient, disciplined, and positive. And as I plugged along, opportunities showed up just when I was prepared to take them on.

But of all the factors that carried me from a dusty Oklahoma farm to the higher reaches of the corporate ladder, the main ingredient was this: Throughout my career I made an effort to learn everything I could about leadership. I'm not an academic. I did not go to business school or study organizational psychology or management in classrooms. I learned in the trenches, by watching good leaders excel and bad leaders mess up and by observing the effects their behavior had on businesses.

The farm I grew up on in the late 1940s and early 1950s had no indoor plumbing. Everyone in the family worked long hours, seven days a week, trying to scrape together a living. Starting when I was eight, I milked a cow every morning before going to class in a one-room schoolhouse. I hauled that milk to our neighbors across the road, Mr. and Mrs. Thompson, who gave me fifty cents, plus some peaches when they were in season—an early lesson in the rewards of good work habits. In the summers, my brother Jerry and I helped out by riding on the back of a hay baler, making sure the bales were tied properly while our grandfather drove the tractor. We considered this fun. Some of our other tasks, like cleaning up the barn after the cows had been milked, we did *not* think of as fun; they were hard work. In fact, I didn't even know about the concept of a vacation until I was in my twenties, when I served meals to vacationers in hotel dining rooms.

Meanwhile, my home life was as unstable as my family's income. By the time I finished high school, my mother had been married four times (she later married once again). But despite that, my mother was rock solid. I didn't realize it at the time, but she was one of the greatest leaders I've ever known: tough and resolute, yet kind and sensitive. She not only was crystal clear about what she expected of my brother and me but also explained *why* she held those standards and made sure we understood the consequences of not living up to them. This is just what a business leader ought to do; that is why I give speeches titled "Manage Like a Mother." The true work of a business leader, like that of a mother, is to help others to be the best they can be. Rather than expect their teams to serve them, good business leaders serve their teams the way mothers serve their children. In turn their people serve their customers better, and excellent business results follow just as surely as solid families follow from solid parenting.

I wish I'd absorbed those leadership lessons better at the time.

I worked part-time throughout my teenage years, doing everything from unloading cement, Sheetrock, and lumber from train cars to delivering prescriptions for the local drugstore. Because the last of my stepfathers was a physician who could afford to send me to college, I was able to enroll at Oklahoma State. I was not the greatest student. I'm more of a hands-on learner, so I learned a lot more through my series of part-time and summer jobs than I ever did in a classroom. As a kitchen steward in my fraternity house I learned about serving people and even more about working with a team.

Realizing that college wasn't for me, I dropped out after two years and joined the army, where I was assigned to cook school. Among the many lessons I learned there was to always have respect for process and procedure—another one of Disney's Great Leader Strategies. One day, while making the dough for three hundred hamburger buns, I did not pay attention to when and how to add the yeast. The result was not pretty. I was demoted to dishwashing and potato-peeling duty for a few days. But this also was a learning opportunity; it taught me how to deal with setbacks and learn from mistakes. Luckily, the electric potato peelers were broken, and I seized the opportunity to get my cook's job back quickly by peeling potatoes better and faster than anyone ever had and by maintaining a positive attitude the whole time.

ENTERING THE HOSPITALITY BUSINESS

I graduated from cook school second in my class. The number one guy was a professional cook from England, my friend Terrence Biggs. I learned a lot from Terrence, including the importance of spending time around people with something to teach.

When our military service drew to a close, Terrence said he'd lined up a job at the new Hilton hotel in Washington, D.C., and could get me one too. Twenty years old with nothing better to do, I seized the opportunity. I'll never forget that first night upon arriving in Washington, when we stayed in an eight-dollar room in a tiny motor hotel called Twin Bridges Marriott. Back then, if anyone had suggested that I'd one day help Marriott grow into a major force in the industry, I'd have called him crazy.

Hilton's personnel manager asked me what kind of job I wanted. I had no idea. I had never set foot in a hotel before. I had never even seen linen napkins, let alone a place setting with more than one fork (in my house you licked off the dinner fork before using it to eat your pie). When the manager offered to make me a banquet waiter, I said "sure," not having any idea what the job was. The closest thing to a banquet I'd ever been to was my high school prom, and that was at the YWCA.

When I saw the grand ballroom, I was so overwhelmed I almost had a heart attack. It seated three thousand people! But my farmer's work ethic and my soldier's discipline got me over the initial hurdles and endeared me to one of the banquet captains, who took me under his wing. He not only taught me how to fold napkins, skirt tablecloths, and pour the right wine into the right glass but also showed me how important it is to train and develop your people, the key leadership principle you'll read about in Chapter Six. He taught me as well the importance of looking and acting like a professional even when I was so exhausted I thought I'd fall asleep on my feet.

Because the guests and my coworkers were from all over the world, my time at the Hilton also taught me about diversity long before social scientists thought up diversity training. The job also taught me a lot about how to treat others. I served presidents, senators, foreign dignitaries, celebrities, and other powerful people. Some of them treated small fry like me like dirt. Others treated us with dignity, and I saw that they were the leaders everyone respected.

It took many years and many mistakes before these invaluable lessons sank in. But my memories of life on the low rungs of the ladder proved extremely valuable when I started thinking about what true leadership is.

I BECOME A MANAGER

After a couple of years as a banquet server, I decided I wanted a more consistent schedule and the kind of experience that could lead to a more stable career. So when I heard about an opening for a clerical job in the food and beverage control office, I applied. It paid only eighty dollars a week, a lot less than I was making. But I wanted the training and those consistent hours, so I waited tables at night in a French restaurant to make my rent. I felt underpaid, underappreciated, and overworked, but because my schedule was so demanding, I learned an awful lot about the importance of being organized. Years later I became known as a proponent and teacher of time management, famous for the use of checklists and my Day-Timer, which still is my best friend.

I'd been a clerk for eight months when the company announced it was looking for management trainees. I was selected, and after a week of training by Jim McGonigle (who ended up being my son's godfather and a lifelong friend), I was made assistant food and beverage controller. I was officially in management, although the total number of people reporting to me was, well, zero.

The best decision I made in that job was to move my office next to the executive chef's. His name was Peter Kleiser, and he was a true teacher who treated everyone with respect. Once, when planning a banquet for three thousand guests, I ordered crenshaw melons instead of honeydews. Instead of reprimanding me or firing me, Peter said, "Lee, you can be a fool once or a fool all your life. When you don't know something, ask questions. Then you'll be a fool only once."

His point: Good leaders are humble enough to admit what they don't know, and *great* leaders are constantly looking for new information. Looking back, I realized why Peter had positioned our office windows so we could see right into the kitchen: That way, the staff and I could get to know each other intimately, and I could constantly learn new things from observing what they were doing. I might have been their boss, but I still had plenty to learn from them. That lesson was more valuable than reading a thousand management books could have been.

I next found myself in Chicago, with a new job, food and beverage controller, at the two-thousand-room Conrad Hilton Hotel. I also had a new wife, Priscilla, whom I had met when we worked together at the Washington Hilton. Her office had been next to mine, and she was always coming in to use my pencil sharpener. I was smitten. After a full year of trying, I finally convinced her to give up her boyfriend and go out with me instead. Forty years, twelve relocations, and a lot of ups and downs later, I'm more grateful than ever that she chose me over him and his little red sports car.

Both my new position and my new marriage helped me learn another important lesson: Your authority—or what you *think* is your authority—is nothing without good relationship skills. At the Conrad Hilton in Chicago I made the mistake of diving right in and trying to change things without first establishing rapport with the executive chef, a man who had held that position since before I was born. He was so annoyed by my arrogance and lack of respect that he banned me from the kitchen. This experience helped me learn that business issues are a lot like a marriage; as Priscilla taught me again and again, you can't resolve conflicts or differences in opinion if your relationship isn't grounded in mutual respect and trust.

NEW YORK, NEW YORK

It was 1969, the year of the moon landing, Woodstock, and the Mets winning the World Series—an incredible time to be in New York for a twenty-five-year-old farm boy. I had become the food and beverage controller at the most famous hotel in New York, maybe even in the world: the legendary Waldorf-Astoria. It was here that I met the man who turned out to be one of the most important figures in my career, my boss, Eugene Scanlon. The Waldorf's rules on performance and professionalism were strict, and Gene not only made them crystal clear but also spelled out the consequences of not following them. Thanks to Gene, I learned that being clear about expectations is exactly what leaders need to do if they want people to perform well. I performed so well I became Gene's assistant a year later.

It was at this point that the value of a true mentor became even more evident. Gene had me attend every banquet and eat in every restaurant in the hotel, so I would learn the fine points of service. Every Monday he took me and another young manager, Bill Wilkinson, to dinner at different restaurants, where he ordered specific foods and wines and explained how special dishes were prepared. He even enrolled me and my coworker and good friend Dennis O'Toole in a wine course and paid for it. His generosity and commitment to my self-improvement reinforced two principles that became central to my approach to work and eventually to the Disney Great Leader Strategies: Train and develop your people, and always look for a better way to do things.

I was in a terrific classroom, but some of the lessons about how to lead other people were slow to sink in. One evening a restaurant guest accused a cocktail server of manipulating the check and overcharging. I marched right up to the server and demanded to see all his guest checks without giving him a chance to defend himself. I'll never forget how his hand shook as he grabbed the Budweiser bottle from his serving tray and smashed it into my face. I needed six stitches above my right eye, which should have taught me a lesson about treating employees—*all employees*—with respect.

Then came a roller coaster of career ups and downs. In 1972 I left the grandeur of the Waldorf for the simple elegance of the Hilton Inn in Tarrytown, New York. As the executive assistant manager and director of food and beverage I was finally in charge of something. The inn had only 205 rooms, but our restaurants were hugely popular, and our patrons were wealthy and demanding. Serving those kinds of people taught me a vital lesson: Some customers may have the power to insist on exceptional service, but *everyone* wants it, and *everyone* deserves it. I liked my new job and my new responsibilities, but my boss was a screamer who treated his employees poorly, so I took a position at another Hilton, only to encounter the same kind of boss. Sick of catering to the whims of a demeaning general manager, I accepted a position at a small hotel in Lancaster, Pennsylvania. Priscilla advised me not to take the job, but I didn't listen. Ninety days later the hotel was bankrupt, and I was out of a job.

It was 1973, and the country was in a recession. Forced to take up residence with Priscilla's parents, I was becoming just about as depressed as the economy when I contacted someone

I'd heard good things about when I was with Hilton. Bud Davis was now vice president of food and beverage at Marriott, and he offered me the position of director of restaurants at the Philadelphia hotel. The company had grown some since that night I had stayed in one of its motels in Washington, but it was still small and relatively unknown, with only thirty-two hotels. Friends in the business tried to talk me out of taking the job; they said Marriott would never be a serious hotel company. But I figured that eating humble pie is better than not eating at all, so I accepted the position. Luckily, my friends were wrong, and it turned out to be a great career decision.

MOVING UP AT MARRIOTT

Over the next seventeen years, I helped Marriott expand to become a giant in the industry. I moved up steadily, and with each new role, my range of influence grew. I earned a reputation as an excellent manager, receiving the highest merit ratings year after year. I was regarded as skilled and extremely well organized and as someone who knew how to make things happen.

One reason I did so well was that I made self-improvement a regular part of my routine. I was constantly listening to tapes and reading books about management. But what proved even more valuable were the vital life lessons I learned on the job. In later positions I got to travel a lot, opening new hotels, and I saw that despite the amazing variety of human beings out there, all everyone wants is to feel special, to be treated with respect, and to be seen as an individual. And the hospitality industry is perfect evidence. Think about it. In hotels and restaurants the customers are not in some distant retail outlet or at the other end of a delivery truck. They're in your face, and they show up in every imaginable mood and physical condition, demanding to be fed, sheltered, and entertained just the way they like it. And the feedback is instantaneous. I sometimes think that everyone should work as a waiter or waitress at some point in his or her life in order to learn these valuable lessons. You have to stay on your toes and excel in customer care, service excellence, and employee relations. As we've learned at the Disney Institute and as you'll see in this book, these principles are not limited to the hospitality industry; they apply just about anywhere you can think of.

Still, as eager as I was to learn the ropes, I never heard a single word at either Hilton or Marriott about leadership responsibility. No one ever explained the difference between managing and leading. I wish someone had; it would have spared me a lot of anguish.

Unfortunately, that beer bottle incident from years ago hadn't been enough to teach me once and for all that intimidation is not the best way to manage people; it might get results in the short run, but it eventually backfires, and it can easily derail a promising career. But it still hadn't sunk in even after a second incident, one involving a troublesome employee who had been accused of making racist remarks. I confronted him, shook my finger in his face, and told him he had a bad attitude. He responded by knocking me out of my chair and cracking me over the head with a clipboard. I guess I'd proved my point about his attitude, but it came at the expense of fourteen new stitches. Priscilla said to me that night, "Lee, do you think this happens because of the way you talk to people?"

She was right, of course, but it took one more incident for the message to truly hit home. When I was area vice president of food and beverage at Marriott, I flew to El Paso, Texas, to visit one of our hotels. To my surprise, the man I was supposed to meet with, the director of food and beverage, was not present. His secretary said he was in the hospital. He'd gotten so stressed out because *Lee Cockerell was coming* that he'd fainted and fallen out of his chair! It was a low point in my life. Was I really that scary? Fortunately, the fellow recovered, and I had dinner with him the next night. He revealed that I had a reputation as a hard-nosed manager who left bodies in his wake. Shortly thereafter I learned why I'd been passed up for a promotion I'd been in line for: I was known for running roughshod over people.

I had a good long talk with myself. I had advanced beyond my wildest dreams because I was a good manager, but it was obvious that my career was dead in its tracks if I didn't change my take-no-prisoners style. So I set out to learn how to *lead,* instead of just manage. I signed up for a three-day leadership conference at the University of Kentucky. I devoured books about great business leaders, as well as public figures who had accomplished miraculous things, like Dr. Martin Luther King, Mahatma Gandhi, and Nelson Mandela. I started seeing leadership lessons everywhere I looked. They blared from the pages of newspapers—the front page, the business section, the sports section, even the entertainment pages—because virtually every problem or conflict in the world can be traced to a leadership failure. I learned to spot great leaders just by watching them and to notice the little things. I saw, for example, that great leaders always focus on others, not on themselves. They hire the right people, train them, trust them, respect them, listen to them, and make sure to be there for them when needed.

When a leader does those things, people step up. It's really that simple. No matter how good your products and services are, you must have committed people at every level who feel involved, appreciated, and proud of what they do. If you treat them well and help them realize their aspirations, they'll work hard and give you their best.

Gradually I began to form these concepts into concrete, action-oriented leadership strategies. In 1988 I became the general manager of a Marriott hotel in Springfield, Massachusetts. It was a small, old, run-down property, but I took the job because I had never been in charge of a hotel before and thought the title would be great for my résumé. But mainly I said yes because the position was a great way to try out the leadership principles I'd learned.

A CHANGE IN LEADERSHIP

My transformation from an autocratic, controlling manager to an inclusive leader yielded immediate dividends in cooperation, motivation, and productivity. The first thing I did in Springfield was to move my office from the fourth floor to the lobby, where my door opened onto the front desk. I left the door open most of the time and told staff to come get me any time they needed me to handle a problem or a guest's complaint. This showed them that I was not only the so-called boss but also part of the team, and it set the tone for a highly successful tenure. When I left in 1990, the frontline employees and managers took up a collection and rented a hall to throw a party for Priscilla and me. Believe me, that felt a whole lot better than having employees hit me over the head or faint at the thought of meeting me, and because employees were happy and motivated, the bottom line was far better served.

So why did I leave? Two words: Disney and France. A Disney executive named Sanjay Varma, with whom I'd worked years before at Marriott, was planning the new Disneyland in Paris. It was scheduled to open in two years, and Sanjay, who is still my good friend, wanted me to put the entire food and beverage operation together.

I had a good life in Springfield. We'd just completed a twelve-million-dollar renovation to the hotel, and it looked great. I had an outstanding team. I was thriving thanks to my new approach to leadership, and I loved that I got to refine my skills every day. Plus I was earning more than the Disney position would pay. So I expected Priscilla to talk me out of it. But she didn't. "Let's go," she said. "If you don't do this, you will look back in five years and be sorry!"

As usual, Priscilla was right; it was an offer I couldn't refuse. Disney was the gold standard in service excellence. In fact, I had even issued a directive at the Springfield Marriott to hire any job applicant who'd ever worked for Disney. Plus my own son, Daniel, had spent the previous summer at the *Walt Disney World*® Resort College Program and raved about the training he received. In the end I couldn't resist Disney's call, and Priscilla couldn't resist Paris. To this day I tell people that my son got me my job at Disney, since he had worked for the company before I did.

From the moment I arrived in France I had to deal with deadline after deadline and boatloads of details in five different languages, all while trying to re-create the Disney culture of excellence, courtesy, and friendliness. For the seven months prior to opening, I worked seventeen hours a day, six or seven days a week. But it all seemed worth it when, on April 12, 1992, we threw an opening night party for ten thousand people. The food alone cost more than a million dollars. We had bought practically every strawberry and shrimp in Europe. It was a huge success, and everyone was thrilled with the great work we had done. We were all geared up and ready for the huge crowds that were forecast for the big opening.

But the crowds never came.

I called it "the summer from Hades." We had a wonderful theme park and great service, but business did not materialize as expected. Money was gushing out, and when revenues go down, stress goes up. Managers and executives were quitting, transferring, and getting fired left and right. I had been in tough circumstances before, and I knew that leaders have to set the proper tone by staying cool, calm, and collected under pressure. No matter what's going on, they have to focus single-mindedly on doing the best they can with what they have instead of blaming, whining, or wishing that things would change. So that's what I did, and three months after the opening, I was promoted to vice president. I was now responsible for the operations of six one-thousand-room resorts.

That was only the beginning of my journey with Disney. After three intense years in Paris, I was transferred to Orlando, Florida, by Judson Green and Al Weiss. As senior vice president of operations for all of the Walt Disney World hotels, I'd now have an opportunity to apply all I'd learned about leadership as an executive at the world's most famous vacation destination. I went home and shouted to Priscilla, "We're going to Disney World!"

Once again the circumstances were challenging. I arrived at Walt Disney World in the middle of a significant business downturn. We were in long meetings almost every night of the week, searching for ways to reduce costs while maintaining Guest satisfaction. During this time I made a special effort to reach out to Cast Members, to get to know them and let them know who I was, how I worked, and what was important to me. I started teaching time management classes, both to help people work more efficiently and to foster good relationships. I scheduled evening meetings for two to three hundred Cast Members at a time, so they could see my face and hear my voice. I invited them to fax me questions and suggestions, and I responded to every one of them. Because of these efforts, we were able to institute smoothly a number of positive changes. In fact, some of the ideas we elicited from Cast Members are still in place today.

Before long I was made executive vice president of operations, responsible for twenty resort hotels with a total of twenty-five thousand rooms, four theme parks, three water parks, and five golf courses, plus shopping, entertainment, and a sports complex, as well as all the ancillary functions of those enterprises. It was in the midst of this, in 1995, that I wrote the Disney Great Leader Strategies. In doing so, I drew upon everything I'd learned along the journey that had got me to where I was: from the ups and downs of dealing with real-life business challenges; from my triumphs and my mistakes; from being treated well and being treated badly; from the bad leaders, good leaders, and outstanding leaders I'd encountered.

Those common sense strategies, which soon became the foundation for the Disney Institute curriculum, served as the guiding light for the rest of my career. But the lessons in leadership didn't end there. I continued to learn every day of my career at Disney, from the Guests we served and the Cast Members I worked with. Even today, as I teach at the Disney Institute and lecture around the world, I continue to learn and grow. As we say at Disney, "In times of drastic change, it is the learners who inherit the future." That is what leading is all about.

CHAPTER THREE

STRATEGY #1

REMEMBER, EVERYONE
IS IMPORTANT

A t *Walt Disney World*® Resort, what is usually known as the laundry is called Textile Services. It consists of three huge separate facilities: one for the more than two million costumes worn by Cast Members; one for the linens used at the 255 food and beverage locations; and the housekeeping plant, which handles the sheets, pillowcases, towels, and washcloths for all the resorts. Cast Members wash, dry, press, and fold 240,000 pounds of linen a day. That's about a million washclothes a week. While many hotels in the business contract their laundry operations to outside companies, Disney has found that doing it all in-house works out to be less expensive and more efficient, thanks mainly to leadership strategies that motivate and empower every single Cast Member to perform to the best of his or her ability.

In the mid-nineties the Textile Services management team attended a three-day seminar about how to include Cast Members at all levels in the decision-making process. Afterward, when the managers announced that the Cast would now be empowered to find ways to enhance teamwork, productivity, and the quality of the final product, the response was not what they had expected. The Cast Members said, basically, "No way!" They thought that if they were put in charge, they'd be blamed and punished when anything went wrong. The message was clear: They didn't trust management.

The managers immediately recognized their mistake: Ironically, in formulating the plan to include more people, they had neglected to consult the very people they sought to empower. So when they regrouped for brainstorming sessions, they made sure to invite a number of Cast Members. The result was an action plan that the Cast happily signed on to and eventually won the approval of skeptical union representatives. Under the new plan, Cast Members would be taught the mission and values of Walt Disney World, learn about the impact of Textile Services on Guest satisfaction measures, be involved in planning for the plant, and participate in a cross-utilization program in which they exchanged jobs with Cast Members in other areas of Walt Disney World. Every aspect of the plan was designed to increase their participation and involvement.

About a year after the new policy was introduced, things were going so well that the Cast was given the freedom and flexibility to set its own productivity targets. The managers reasoned that the Cast would make smarter decisions if it knew exactly how its work affected the budget process and the company's bottom line. At the time, allowing frontline Cast Members to set their own productivity numbers was unheard of, because management assumed they would set the bar way too low. But most departments actually set their numbers very *high*, even when we said they would be held accountable for meeting their goals. The result? They blew us away! Their productivity far exceeded management's expectations.

It took hard work and a good deal of retraining, but the reinvention of Textile Services quickly yielded measurable results, not only in productivity but also in innovation and employee satisfaction. Cast Members continued to come up with fresh ways to improve their work, finding creative solutions to problems that management alone could never have dreamed of. You'll read about some of those later in the book. Over time the turnover rate at Textile Services dropped steadily; today the operation loses only 5 to 7 percent of its full-time staff a year, remarkably low for any organization and especially low among employees doing physically demanding work. The Textile Services section is now one of the crown jewels of the company, showcased at the Disney Institute as a shining example of the impact a great leadership strategy can have.

TRUE INCLUSION

The transformation of Textile Services is a prime example of the first and most important leadership principle, inclusion. "Inclusion" is a major buzzword in business today. It's usually thought of in terms of ethnic, racial, religious, and gender diversity and filling the workplace with representatives of every demographic category. This is an important and worthy endeavor, and I'm proud that during my tenure at Walt Disney World we created an environment that welcomed Cast Members of every culture, religion, gender, race, ethnicity, physical condition, and sexual orientation. But inclusion is not just a matter of hiring policy or of respecting the differences among people from diverse cultures and backgrounds. It's about engaging and involving your employees and showing them that each one of them is important. On the surface, a workplace can look as diverse as the United Nations, but if the employees are not truly respected, not truly valued, not truly involved, and not truly treated with dignity, what you have is a great photo opportunity, not real inclusion.

The reason inclusion is so important is simple: When *everyone matters and everyone knows he or she matters*, employees are happy to come to work, and they're eager to give you their energy, creativity, and loyalty. The result is predictable: more productivity and satisfaction; less absenteeism and turnover. On the other hand, when people don't feel included, they become apathetic and perform at less than their full capacity. To put it simply, all people want exactly what you want. You want to be included, listened to, respected, and involved, don't you? You want to be asked your opinion and have it taken seriously. You want to feel valued. And you want to be known as an individual and treated as such. Well, so does everyone else. That's why great leaders make sure that everyone in the workplace—no matter the rank or position—feels included and no one feels left out.

At Disney we defined our approach to inclusion with the acronym RAVE: respect, appreciate, and value everyone. If you respect, appreciate, and value your employees, the word will get out. As a result, people will line up to work for you, and current employees will not want to leave. That's exactly what happened at Walt Disney World when we began to implement the Great Leader Strategies; Cast Members convinced their friends and family to move to Orlando and apply for jobs. It's also why the company has the lowest turnover rate of any major company in the hospitality industry.

I'm proud that during my tenure at Disney I earned a reputation as an inclusive leader. Dieter Hannig, whom I promoted to senior vice president of food and beverage, once told a magazine: "Lee can relate to all people at all levels, no matter what their background is, from the pot washer from Santo Domingo to the maid from Haiti. He has the ability to touch them and reach them. It's a gift." I mention this not to blow my own horn but because Dieter was wrong. The ability he described is not a gift. It's a learned behavior. As I pointed out earlier, relating well to people was not always part of my skill set. I learned through painful lessons how to treat *everyone* with respect and dignity. I worked hard at it and eventually mastered it. Then I helped teach it to other leaders.

You too can create a culture of inclusion in your organization or group by applying the following strategies. They will show you how to foster an environment in which your employees are engaged, motivated, and fully committed to the goals of your organization, just as we did at Disney.

1. Make sure everyone matters . . . and that everyone knows it. Business leadership is a lot like parenting: Your job is not just to make your employees happy but to create an environment that enables them to excel at what they do. Just as great parents pay attention to everyone in their family, so great leaders pay attention to everyone in their organizations, bolstering his or her self-esteem and self-confidence at every step. If everyone feels recognized, appreciated, and listened to, everyone will want to take every opportunity to learn and grow.

In my years at Disney I constantly trumpeted this basic idea: Every single Cast Member is important to our company. I didn't just do it as a motivational device or a way to gain popularity. It was a no-nonsense business practice with an immediate payoff. When people feel valued for the talents and skills they bring to the team, their level of commitment soars. And committed people feel a strong personal connection to, and responsibility for, the work that they do and the teams they're a part of. As a result, you'll be able to recruit and retain the best and most dedicated employees, keeping turnover, disciplinary problems, and absenteeism low. Common sense? Yes. Common practice? No.

The principle that everyone matters also has another clear advantage: It's true! If any job were *unimportant*, why would you bother to hire someone to do it? As you can imagine, the quality of french fries at Walt Disney World is an important element in Guest satisfaction. Who do you think is more important, the person who calculates how many potatoes to order, the person who places the order with the supplier, the person who unloads the cartons, the one who fries the potatoes, or the one who serves the cooked french fries? The answer I always gave the Cast Members was: They're *all* equally important. If any one of them doesn't do his or her job, the Guest won't have a satisfying experience, and business will suffer. I learned that lesson early in my career, when I worked as the grease man in Harvey's Hotel and Casino at Lake Tahoe, Nevada. I spent my time pushing a little cart around the kitchens, emptying grease from the griddles, and I was treated with disdain. But I realized that without me the grills would shut down, as the holders overflowed with hot grease. No grease man, no hamburgers; no hamburgers, no customers; no customers, no restaurant.

My point is this: The people who clean the bathrooms, sweep the floors, and empty the garbage are just as important as the executives, managers, directors, and supervisors. Maybe even *more* important. Ditto the ticket takers, the parking lot attendants, and the people who answer the phones. Imagine how many of the Guests at Disney World might vacation someplace else if the bathrooms and floors were dirty or if the people responsible for creating a Guest's first impressions were rude or unhelpful. *Everyone* is important. And this is not just true of theme parks and resorts; it is true of every organization everywhere, including yours.

2. Know your team. If you have children—or godchildren or nieces and nephews—you know how important it is to treat each one in a way that makes him or her feel special. You probably also know that the way to make one child feel special may not be the way to make another feel special. As a parent, you find it easy to treat each child as an individual because you've discovered over time what makes each of them unique and how to appreciate him or her for who he or she is. Why not do the same with your employees and team members?

Every worker has different motivations, priorities, preferences, and dreams. Workers hail from different backgrounds and different neighborhoods. To make them feel special, you have to get to know every person. How do you do that? Learn about your employees' past work experiences, their aspirations, their skills and talents, their short- and long-term goals. Get to know about their personal interests and their families as well. They'll light up when you remember some seemingly minor fact about their lives. Now, take it one step further: Use that information to find ways to maximize their abilities and help them realize their goals and ambitions.

When I worked at Walt Disney World and had to meet with one of the managers who reported to me, I'd often go to his or her office. Some might expect that since I was the boss, the proper procedure would have been for him or her to come to me. But reversing the protocol gave me the opportunity to get to know each one better and to become familiar with his or her coworkers. You can learn an awful lot about employees from the photos on their desks, the artworks on their walls, and the way they interact with the people around them.

Getting to know each person as an individual isn't easy, and it doesn't happen overnight. But believe me, it pays off big-time. (We'll revisit this important subject in another context, in Chapter Eight.)

3. Let your team get to know you. Remember, your inclusive workplace includes you. Too many leaders keep their distance from employees, both physically and emotionally. Believing that they can't manage well unless they project an image of impervious strength, they hide their humanity, especially their flaws and weaknesses. I promise you, you'll get a lot more respect if you let people know who you really are.

That doesn't mean you should broadcast your deepest, darkest secrets. But make sure the people around you know what moves you, what excites you, what you care deeply about, and even what you struggle with. This holds especially for owning up to your mistakes and admitting what you don't know. These are some of the hardest things for leaders to do; many are afraid it will undermine their authority or cause people to lose confidence in them and their abilities. But I've found that the opposite is true: The more authentic you are, the more your employees and peers will respect you and the more they will trust your judgment. Believe me, they already know you're a human being, and they already know you make mistakes, so no amount of posturing is going to convince them otherwise. They'll respect you more if they sense that you are being candid and genuine.

Whether you're looking up or down the corporate ladder, make sure you treat everyone you interact with the same way, with respect. If you don't, people will see you as a phony, and you'll lose credibility. I'm sure you've seen leaders who act totally differently when their bosses are around from when they're in front of their direct reports. Didn't some red flags go up as soon as you saw the difference? If you ever find yourself behaving differently around different people, stop yourself. That's another lesson I learned the hard way.

Early in my career I found it difficult to juggle my behavior when my bosses and my direct reports were all in the same room. But life as a leader got a whole lot easier when I started being myself twenty-four hours a day, for better or for worse. If you learn to do this and have the confidence to do it consistently, people will say good things about you—to your face and behind your back—and your effectiveness as a manager and an employee will soar. Most workplaces are way too full of people who take themselves too seriously. Take your *responsibility*, not yourself, seriously.

4. Greet people sincerely. Many tough-minded leaders sneer at this advice because it sounds like something a mother would say when she sends her child to school. Some leaders get so wrapped up in their work and in projecting a commanding image that they walk right past people without acknowledging them or, worse yet, acknowledging only *some* of them—usually the same ones day in and day out. I assure you, if you walk past people as if they were invisible, everyone will notice, and it will send a demoralizing message about how little you value them. Never underestimate the power of a simple gesture like saying hello or stopping to chat for a minute or two. And make sure you mean it; if you're just going through the motions like a glad-handing politician looking for votes, they'll see right through you. As the old saying goes, "People will not remember what you said, but they will remember how you made them feel."

On my frequent strolls around Walt Disney World, I always stopped to say hello to as many Cast Members as I could. I'll never forget the looks on their faces when I asked how their husbands or wives were or when I remembered where they had been born or that a child had recently gone off to college. I also remember the wounded expression of an employee who told me that her manager of ten years did not know whether she had a son or a daughter. It would have made a tremendous difference to that woman's work performance if her boss had shown a genuine interest in her family.

5. Reach out to everyone on your team. Everyone wants to be heard and respected. It's one of our most basic human needs. But hearing all voices is not just vital for building morale and self-confidence; it's a crucial source of information for you as a leader. Great leaders know they don't know everything. They learn as they go, and they're confident enough to listen to people at every level of their organizations. As a result, they make better choices and fewer mistakes. They also inspire greater commitment to and more support for their decisions. By reaching out to everyone on your team, you gain the benefit of a variety of perspectives. Make it clear that you want to hear from everyone, whatever his or her title or position, and that you want everyone to speak his or her mind. Ask for people's opinions and ideas even if they don't volunteer them.

Never underestimate the wisdom and resourcefulness of your frontline staff. After all, they're the ones in the trenches day after day, seeing things you don't see and picking up information you can't possibly have. Ask them direct questions, such as "Is this the best way to get this done?" and "Is there anything else I should know before I make this decision?" Let them know you appreciate their advice, even when it is the opposite of what you were thinking or something you disagree with or might not want to hear. Remember, they're probably intimidated by your position, so put them at ease, and thank them for being honest with you. How many times have you heard leaders say, after a crisis has erupted, "Why didn't anyone tell me?" Probably they were afraid to. They'll tell you the truth only if they trust you 100 percent.

Over the years I've seen countless examples of how involving people at all levels leads to continual improvement in productivity, innovation, and problem solving, and I'll share many of them throughout the book. Once, for example, in an attempt to reduce the cost of room amenities in one of Disney World's resort hotels, management decided to eliminate the free sewing kits we placed in each room. It reasoned that no one really used or needed them and that the Guests probably wouldn't even notice they were missing. Well, the Guests *did* notice, and you wouldn't believe the firestorm that resulted. You see, those kits came in tin boxes decorated with beautiful Victorian images. The Guests didn't want them for sewing; they liked taking them home as souvenirs. The problem was, the managers had not bothered to ask the opinion of the housekeepers, the ones who *really* knew what room amenities Guests wanted. The housekeepers set us straight, and the sewing kits were quickly returned to the rooms. If we had asked the experts in the first place, we would never have made that mistake.

The next time you go to a Walt Disney World Resort, pay attention to the service you receive and the way you and your family are treated. Chances are you'll notice something special, something you might not see at other hotels, restaurants, or theme parks. And chances are the original idea came from a person or a team that was fairly low on the totem pole. For example, at Disney World you'll see a different family get selected to open the park each morning. You'll see bus drivers break out in song as they ferry you back to your resort late at night when everyone is exhausted. You'll see security hosts and hostesses singling out children to be deputy security hosts, complete with a ceremony in which they raise their right hands and take an oath to have a good time. All those ideas came from Cast Members.

Chances are you'll make a point of eating at the Whispering Canyon Café in the Wilderness Lodge. Be warned, it's a noisy place. The servers are loud; they shout out funny things and sometimes make teasing remarks to the Guests. Then, when you least expect it, one of them will round up all the kids and lead them on a make-believe horseback ride around the restaurant. Songs can break out at any moment. It's all part of the show, and children love it. Where did the concept come from? Not from upper management, I can assure you. It came from the Cast Members when the lodge first opened. It was a strange idea at the time, but the leaders were smart enough to listen. Whispering Canyon has since become one of the most popular restaurants at Disney World, and the Wilderness Lodge has since been rated the top family-friendly hotel in the country.

6. Make yourself available. Do everything in your power to be there for people when they need you. Like good parents, great leaders are always available. At Disney, I let all the Cast Members know that I was available to anyone who wanted to see me about anything, and I made good on that promise by making time for everyone who requested a meeting, regardless of his or her position in the organization. Some executives fear that a policy like that will take up too much of their time. I found that it *saved* time, because it helped create a happier, more productive environment and because it prevented a lot of problems that would have completely devoured my time. In fact, far fewer people than you might expect actually made appointments to see me, but just knowing that they could had a powerful effect. And when they did come to see me, the impact was usually profound.

Because they knew I would give them a fair hearing and follow through on my commitments, frontline Cast Members and managers came to me directly with their concerns and complaints. Some, for example, thought that they were not being given an opportunity to get into management. Others came because they were having difficulty with managers and wanted advice on what to do. By helping them resolve these concerns before they festered into resentment and antagonism, we made the workplace more harmonious and we kept many competent people who might otherwise have left. And sometimes my open-door policy unearthed vital information, like the time a Cast Member felt safe enough to tell me that a coworker was taking food from the company and reselling it. "I know you'll take care of it," she said, and I did, quickly and quietly.

On some occasions I'd be told about personal concerns that were not work-related at all. A Cast Member from one of our resort pastry shops came to me once and said that her mother had fallen and needed a walker. She could not afford to buy one because she had spent all her money installing ramps in her house and repairing the damage from a recent hurricane. Because I'd said that anyone could come to me if he or she ever needed anything, she asked for help. I contacted the United Way, and a few days later there was a walker on that Cast Member's porch. It had taken me less than half an hour to get her that walker, and the payoff in loyalty and motivation was incalculable.

Many leaders think it's a waste of time to listen to the problems of low-level employees. I don't. I learned over the course of my career that if you take care of all the little issues, big problems are less likely to occur. Because I was available, I could resolve delicate issues quickly, before they escalated, and the company was spared some protracted grievances and legal entanglements. And because I worked hard at being available, other Disney leaders followed my example, and the practice became commonplace at every level of the operation.

So let your team know you're there for them when they need you. That means twenty-four hours a day, so give them the appropriate phone numbers and let them know it's really OK to use them. Yes, it's a pain to get calls at home, and it's awful to be awakened in the middle of the night. But it comes with the territory, and it won't kill you. In my experience, people rarely abuse the privilege, so the calls you do get are likely to be of great importance. Moreover, merely making the gesture sends a strong signal that you really do want to hear from everyone, at any time. Your employees may never use your home number, but just knowing they have it will make them far more willing to come to your office or send you an e-mail with information you need to know.

When something of concern to one of your people comes up, try to see him or her as soon as you can. That's the reason I include this essential tip in my time management seminars: Always leave blank spaces in your calendar to accommodate the unexpected, because the unexpected is often more important than the expected.

7. **Listen to understand.** Making yourself available is an empty gesture unless you genuinely listen. As Stephen Covey puts it in *The 7 Habits of Highly Effective People*, "Seek first to understand, then to be understood." Too many leaders fail to stay focused on the person they're speaking with because they're thinking about something else or rehearsing what they're going to say next. Their body language practically screams, "Shut up!" Good leaders, on the other hand, take the time to let people express their thoughts completely. Yes, this requires patience. Yes, people often ramble on and on out of nervousness and take forever to get to the point. Yes, they often tell you what you already know. But it's vital to hang in there, because you never know when a glimmer of an idea might shine through. The sentence you tuned out on might hold a crucial fact or reveal an important problem you need to know about. And even if you learn nothing newsworthy, listening to people speak their minds tells them that you care about what they have to say.

There is another reason to give the speaker your full attention: Most often what people are saying and what they are *trying* to say are two different things. There is much to be learned from body language and from what is being left out. But in order to read between the lines, you have to stay focused, so allow no distractions or interruptions from phone calls, paperwork, or text messaging. As you're listening, you might want to take notes to refer to later; even the best leaders can't always remember everything. And when the person is finished speaking, it's a good idea to reiterate what he or she has said, to make sure you've understood. Say, "I think you are saying . . ." or "I understand from what you said that what you want me to do is . . ." or "Is there anything else that you think I should know?" Showing that you are trying hard to grasp what they are saying will put people at ease, and that will encourage them to speak openly and candidly. As a result, you will dramatically improve your odds of learning the whole truth.

Speaking of putting people at ease, here's a tip that worked really well for me. When Cast Members came to see me in my office, I went out and greeted them myself rather than had my assistant bring them to me. I sat beside them in the same kind of chairs they were in, not in the big comfortable chair behind my desk. In fact, the only times I *ever* sat behind my desk were when I was alone. When the meeting ended, I always escorted my visitors out of my office and thanked them for coming over. In other words, I didn't just make the time to see them; I made an effort to show them I was really there.

By the way, I always held the door open for my visitors, and I held it until they got all the way through—just as my mother had taught me when I was a boy. It was a basic lesson in courtesy that I always remembered, and as a leader I practiced it both literally and metaphorically by using my authority to open doors for people so they could reach their highest potentials.

8. Communicate clearly, directly, and honestly. Good communication is *clear* communication. Use ordinary language, and say exactly what you mean. If you don't, people will leave more confused than they were before, and you'll pay the price in inefficiency and loss of trust. Beating around the bush increases confusion, not clarity. If you "spin" your message, people will see right through it, and their trust in you will be undermined, perhaps forever. If you communicate clearly, directly, and honestly all the time, people will understand what you want them to know and what you want them to do. And you will earn a reputation as a trustworthy individual. People may not always like what you say, but at least they will trust that you mean it. Nothing is more important if you want to be a great leader.

Make an effort to communicate one-on-one in person when-ever you can. Nothing makes people feel more valued than a face-to-face meeting. Second best is a one-on-one phone con-versation; if that isn't possible, try gathering people in small groups. If you must resort to e-mail or written notes, find a way to personalize those messages, and try to make them enjoyable and interesting. Yes, this takes time and effort—no one said good communication was easy—but the payoff is enormous.

9. Stand up for the excluded. Be on the lookout for people who feel left out for one reason or another, such as a new em-ployee eating lunch alone in the cafeteria. If someone is being excluded socially, it usually has nothing to do with his or her skills, but the isolation *will* affect his or her performance. Maybe the person is shy and finds it difficult to speak up. Maybe he or she looks or sounds different from everyone else and has been made to feel insecure in the group. Maybe he or she grew up in an unfamiliar culture and coworkers are uneasy about how to relate to him or her. There are a million reasons a person can feel excluded in the workplace, but whatever the underlying cause may be, the instant it comes to your atten-tion, take steps to rectify the situation. Make sure your team understands how important it is that everyone on the team—re-gardless of race, religion, gender, sexual orientation, or physi-cal appearance—feels included, and always set a good example yourself.

Make no mistake, anyone who *feels* left out *is* left out. I learned that lesson in my very first job. There I was, fresh out of the army, a country boy from Oklahoma working at a fancy ho-tel in the nation's capital. All the other waiters were profes-sionals who had been trained at the best facilities in Europe. Not only had I not been formally trained anywhere, but I also hadn't even finished college. I felt so totally left out that I was tempted to get on the first bus back to Oklahoma. It was a huge blow to my self-esteem and self-confidence, and it affected my ability to do my job.

Luckily, my supervisor, Kurt, made me feel as if I belonged. Not only that, but he took me under his wing and helped transform me from a timid kid who had no idea why a table setting needs more than one fork and thought that Sterno (the fuel used for heating up chafing dishes) was an appetizer into a confident young man who couldn't wait to learn the next new thing. Kurt was tough. He insisted that everything be done perfectly. But despite my frequent mistakes, he never made me feel dumb, and he never embarrassed me in front of others. He just quietly told me the right way to do things. I never forgot Kurt's example.

10. Forget about the chain of command. The days of the vertical chain of command as a way of doing business are over. Leaders who continue to manage this way are doomed to failure, because a rigid top-down command structure can slow communication significantly and deliver less than reliable information. This is especially true of emotionally charged issues, because feelings are never translated or passed on properly in a command chain. This doesn't mean that people should not talk first to their immediate supervisors when problems arise; it means that good leaders are willing to listen to anyone in their organizations, whether or not that person reports to them directly.

I think it is fine for leaders to make it clear to their reports exactly what they want to be informed of and how they expect information to be presented. But there should never be a hint of intimidation. There is no room for such comments as "Why did you talk to him before talking with me?" At Walt Disney World, Al Weiss and I learned to work with a flexible chain of command over the years. My direct reports talked directly to Al or to whomever else they thought appropriate whenever they needed to, and they would leave me a voice mail summarizing the discussion or else update me later on. I attribute much of our success to that style of leadership, because the message it sent was: "We trust you to do the right thing, and we are confident you'll make the right choices."

Needless to say, this kind of flexibility requires an enormous amount of trust, but once that trust has been established, and fear has been removed from the equation, you'll find that information is far more likely to flow where it's needed when it's needed.

11. Don't micromanage. If you want to lose great people quickly, look over their shoulders all the time and make all their decisions for them. On the other hand, if you want to be a great leader, learn to let go. Hire great people, be perfectly clear about their responsibility, authority, and accountability, and let them do their thing. You may earn more money than they do, and you may have a fancier title, but none of that makes you smarter than your direct reports. Whenever I needed to remind someone of that, I would tell them about the button I once saw on the shirt of Ken Blanchard, the leadership and management expert. It read, "None of us is as smart as all of us."

Yes, there are times of crisis when a leader needs to take command. But it's the height of arrogance to assume that every difficult situation needs you to take over and make every decision. In fact, the opposite may be true. In Chapter Four, you'll read about what we went through at Walt Disney World on September 11, 2001, and in the immediate aftermath. In the midst of that terrible crisis, everyone came through with flying colors precisely because we *shared* the leadership role as the situation required.

12. Design your culture. The Disney Institute defines a corporate culture as "the system of values and beliefs an organization holds that drives actions and behaviors and influences relationships." Whether you recognize it or not, your organization has one. So the question isn't whether you have a corporate culture but what kind of culture you have. Does it work for you or against you? Successful cultures are established by design, not by chance, and they're clear, well defined, and purposeful. One of those purposes should be to create and foster an inclusive environment. It has never been more crucial for leaders to promote, in word and deed, inclusiveness at every level of their operation.

There is no downside to designing a culture of inclusiveness; it is 100 percent upside for every part of your business and frankly for our country and the whole world. I've seen its impact in organizations of every size and shape, from corporate giants like Disney to mom-and-pop operations. For instance, Laurie Kotas, founder and CEO of Wishland, a small nonprofit in Southern California that works with wish-granting organizations to provide assistance and cherished moments to seriously ill children and their families, says that after taking a Disney Institute seminar, she realized "the importance of defining and creating a culture that can be in place as the organization grows, and where everyone feels they're an important part of our magic and success." Once she started communicating her refined vision of an inclusive, mission-driven organization, she got an immediate buy-in from her staff of three, her board, and her corps of volunteers. The result was a boost of enthusiasm, commitment, and creative ideas, as well as an increase in volunteers and donations.

On the other end of the spectrum is the international auto giant Volvo. Kevin Meeks, the network and business development director at Volvo's British operation (Volvo Car UK Limited), says that "one of the most important learnings from our time with Disney was a deeper appreciation of the role that every individual in the company plays in delivering an outstanding service to our customers." This realization inspired the company to revise its employee training program. The result is what it calls Volvo PRIDE, an acronym for passion, respect, integrity, drive, and energy. Highlighting Volvo's culture, heritage, and reputation for safety, quality, and environmental care, the program is rated as "very good" or "outstanding" by 95 percent of its attendees. "It creates a passion for the brand and demonstrates how individuals can personally contribute to the success of the business," says Meeks. "We know that Volvo PRIDE is helping to strengthen our brand and customer experience."

However you measure success, designing an inclusive culture will surely yield results in your organization. But this doesn't mean it's easy. In fact, it's a journey that never ends, and it's a prime example of something I said earlier: The soft stuff is actually the hard stuff. Managers often say they have no time for the soft stuff because they're busy with the "important" things: making money, increasing productivity, cutting costs, enforcing rules, keeping labor in line, and the rest of the measurable tasks that running a business requires. But the fact is, if you don't do the soft stuff well, you will never achieve the payoff you're aiming for with the hard stuff. That's why it pays to take care of your people before you take care of your paperwork.

13. Treat your people as you would want your customers to be treated. The bottom line of this chapter is that there is a direct correlation between how you treat your employees and how those employees treat your customers. Cast Members at Walt Disney World are trained to deliver on these Four Guest Expectations:

- * Make me feel special.

- * Treat me as an individual.

- * Respect me and my children.

- * Be knowledgeable.

That's basically what customers of any business want, over and above a high-quality product. Disney leadership trains Cast Members to fulfill these expectations by treating *them* the same way. You might call it Disney's version of the Golden Rule: Leaders do unto Cast Members the way they want Cast Members to do unto Guests. It works because the Four Cast Expectations are essentially the same.

- * Make me feel special.

- * Treat me as an individual.

- * Respect me.

- * Make me knowledgeable.

Your employees have the same four expectations; if you fulfill them, their self-esteem and confidence will soar, and they'll behave in a professional and caring way. And you know what follows from that: bottom line business results. I can't emphasize this enough. In studying the Guest satisfaction surveys at Walt Disney World, I've seen a clear trend: People who say they had a memorable interaction with a Cast Member invariably give an excellent rating, and they are also far more likely to return on their next vacation.

By the way, the same reasoning applies to employees who do not have direct contact with customers. Treat them properly, and those "backstage" workers will treat suppliers, direct reports, supervisors, and one another properly. It's simple human nature: If you want people to behave a certain way, model it by treating them that same way.

At Walt Disney World, I and other leaders did our best to make every last member of the Cast feel trusted and respected, while the Cast Members did all they could to make kids feel important and parents feel valued. Without that, Walt Disney World might not have remained the most popular tourist destination in the world. The same formula can help you and your business achieve similar success.

ACTION STEPS

* Ask yourself frequently what you have done to show that everyone is important and knows it.

* Create an environment that makes every employee and every customer feel special.

* Treat everyone as an individual.

* Give every person your complete and unconditional respect.

* Spend time getting to know your employees.

* Give every employee the information and resources to learn what he or she needs to know and acquire the skills he or she needs to have.

* Make yourself truly available to everyone on your team.

* Give everyone, regardless of his or her position, the opportunity to be heard.

* When someone speaks to you, give that person your complete attention and really listen.

* Be your authentic self; don't project a false persona.

CHAPTER FOUR

STRATEGY #2

BREAK THE MOLD

W hen I moved to France to help create Disneyland Paris, I soon learned that our success would depend largely on the quality of our restaurants. After all, Europeans love their food, so the twenty full-service, high-end eateries in our hotels and entertainment centers would be judged by very discerning palates. I knew that the key to success would be to hire world-class restaurant chefs and restaurant managers. There was only one problem: Professionals of that stature typically don't like working in hotels. I'd learned from trying unsuccessfully to recruit some of them that they are artists and that kitchens and dining rooms are their studios. And, like all artists, they are at their creative best when left alone. They can't stand administrators looking over their shoulders telling them what to do and how to do it, and since that's what they often find in large hotels and resorts, they almost always prefer to work in freestanding restaurants.

I started to wonder how a huge operation like ours could give culinary artists the freedom and authority they needed to create a world-class dining experience. Then it dawned on me: Maybe it was a structural issue. Typically, hotel chefs and restaurant managers report to a food and beverage director, who in turn reports to the hotel's general manager. But creative chefs kept telling me that food and beverage directors are too controlling. I couldn't disagree since I had been a food and beverage director myself and I'd often overruled good ideas because of cost concerns or fear of deviating from standard practice. Well, what if we broke the mold and eliminated that middle layer? Maybe if the chefs and restaurant managers reported directly to the general manager, they'd have the autonomy they thrive on. With less bureaucratic interference, they could make creative decisions about menus and ambience and have the authority to hire whomever they wanted. And in situations where upper management had to be consulted, they would be part of the process. The structural change would also send a message to everyone in the company that chefs and restaurant managers were not just puppets of the food and beverage directors; they were decision makers who were to be treated as vital members of the team.

It was a huge structural change for Disney and extremely unorthodox for the resort business in general, and it turned out to be one of the best decisions I ever made. From then on I could tell top chefs and managers that working at Disney would be like working in an independent restaurant, where the only person they answered to was the owner. As a result, we got the talent we needed, and that talent got an environment that allowed it to do its best work. When the resorts opened, reviewers said that our food was as outstanding as that of any fine Parisian restaurant.

Experiences like that made me vividly aware of a crucial component of leadership: organizational structure. You might hire the best possible people, inspire them, and pay them every cent they're worth, but if you don't give them the right framework in which to operate, they can't perform at their best. On the other hand, if you structure your workplace to maximize your employees' creative potential, you'll have a major competitive advantage. No matter what business or organization you're in, when it comes to structure, you have to be willing to break the mold.

Your job as a leader is to figure out what the organization *should* look like, not just to do your best within the existing design. Unfortunately, many leaders consider organizational details boring, and others don't think structural changes are worth all the hard work. But I can assure you, good organizational architecture not only keeps costs in line and maximizes efficiency but also streamlines the decision-making process, enhances employee satisfaction, and facilitates creativity and innovation at all levels.

REIMAGINING WALT DISNEY WORLD

Although improving the reporting structure of the Disney restaurants proved to be a very positive structural change, it was a relatively small one. Two years after I transferred to *Walt Disney World*® Resort in Orlando, Al Weiss and I (with the support of our boss, Judson Green) were called upon to completely overhaul the organizational structure. The idea was to improve dramatically the operations of the theme parks and resorts. Ever since the Orlando facility opened in 1971, Parks and Resorts had been run as two separate organizations, each with its own executive team, finance group, human resources department, and so on. As you can imagine, duplication of effort was commonplace, and good ideas were seldom shared between the groups. People worked in one division or the other, and hardly anyone crossed over. The managers in Parks were so out of touch with their counterparts in Resorts that they might as well have worked for different companies.

When I first arrived in Orlando, I heard stories like the following. Thomas Katheder, now a vice president in the legal department, began his Disney career as an attorney in 1990. After completing the weeklong orientation program for new employees, Thomas and the other participants were escorted into an adjacent room and told to form a queue. "As I came to the head of the line," he recalls, "a woman behind a table asked me, 'Parks or Resorts?' She was handing out tiny brass pins with Disney icons emblazoned on them. We were supposed to attach one to our nametags to identify ourselves as an employee of either Parks or Resorts. I explained that as a member of the legal department I would support *both* divisions. 'Parks or Resorts?' she intoned again. I quickly snatched one of each pin and scurried away. As I drove back to my office, I wondered if I had made the right decision in moving nearly a thousand miles to work for Disney."

Fortunately for the company, Thomas stayed on and distinguished himself. So did a lot of others who wondered privately about the wisdom of keeping the two divisions separate. It was not the most efficient use of resources and brainpower, but because the company's financial results were solid and Guest satisfaction was high, nobody in charge had seen the need to change the structure. Judson, Al, and I had fresh eyes. Our primary objective was to empower all Cast Members and make the most of their talents, and we saw that making the lines of responsibility, authority, and accountability sharper would greatly improve our chances of succeeding. So we decided to place Parks and Resorts under a single umbrella, with everyone reporting up to Al.

At first, consolidating the two divisions triggered resistance and caused some pain. It altered the career paths of a number of managers, who were not at all pleased. And yes, we lost some good people. Some did not like their new assignments, others couldn't accept reporting to someone who had previously been their peer, and yet others felt insecure about their future. But the job loss was minimal, and no one who stayed lost a penny of his or her salary. As for the great majority of Cast Members, the change proved to be a tremendous boon. Bright new career horizons opened up for everyone because people could now move freely between positions in Parks and Resorts. Young Cast Members could gain a wider range of experience early in their careers, and people who had been working in the same department for many years could try new things. A centralized system was created to move people around and give Cast Members cross-training in areas they wanted to experience. Before, someone in Parks wouldn't even have known about an opening in Resorts, let alone been invited to apply for it. Now during the Christmas rush and other busy times for the hotels someone in park maintenance could try working in a resort kitchen, or a resort housekeeper could enjoy the company of excited children by working in a quick service restaurant at the Magic Kingdom.

There was also greater potential for career advancement, as ambitious people could now seize opportunities in either division. Mim Flynn and Liz Clark are good examples of this. Under the old system, as a manager at the Magic Kingdom, Liz didn't have many opportunities to be promoted within the

Parks division. But now she was able to move into a higher position, managing food operations at Disney's Wide World of Sports, which used to be in the Resorts division. She did a great job and gained valuable experience, and then was able to return to the Magic Kingdom in an even higher role as senior executive in charge of food. The person she replaced was Mim Flynn, who had worked in the Parks division her whole career and was now promoted to senior executive in charge of food and beverage in Resorts, where her park experience proved valuable. The moves that enabled both women's careers to blossom would not have been possible if we hadn't changed the organizational structure. They are still two of Disney's most valued executives.

As you can see, the new structure gave management far more ways to utilize individual talent. People could now be moved around to provide help where it was most needed. For example, hotel restaurants are extremely busy at breakfast and slow at lunch, and it's just the reverse in the parks. Now a Cast Member could work the breakfast shift in a hotel and help out in a park restaurant at lunchtime. The company could also more rapidly adjust to unanticipated fluctuations in business. When it rained, for instance, and thousands of Guests dashed from the parks to the hotels, we could quickly redeploy park employees to lend a hand. Plus we saved a whole lot of money by eliminating unnecessary duplication; we now had only one executive with one support staff for each department instead of two and one set of procedures for training instead of two different ones.

Of course it took some time to set the new structure in place, but it soon seemed as natural to the Disney way of life as the increase in Guests every summer when school lets out. It also proved to be a crucial factor in the steady upward trend in the company's fortunes since the mid-1990s. But we didn't rest on our laurels. In May 1997 we broke the mold again. Up until then all the support groups—purchasing, security, transportation, and maintenance—had been separate from the operating groups. Operations reported to me, and support reported to one of my peers. We realized that things would get done far more quickly and effectively if both groups were placed within a single framework, with the support groups reporting to me directly.

Having fewer kingdoms and fewer kings quickly led to better results. No longer did one executive have to negotiate with another executive over every major decision. In the past, for example, if I wanted to add more security to a certain location, I had to negotiate with my counterpart in support to convince him to rework his budgets and staff assignments. Or if the bus drivers suggested that certain routes run every fifteen minutes instead of thirty, or the housekeepers asked for more of a certain product, I couldn't just approve the requests. I had to work through the support division because it handled transportation and purchasing. But once we consolidated operations and support, I could make the needed adjustments with a quick phone call or two, instead of tedious negotiations and long waiting periods.

Pretty soon the structure of Walt Disney World was completely revamped. Instead of separate domains with fuzzy boundaries, we had a clear structure that enabled us to make faster decisions, manage costs more efficiently, streamline our processes and procedures, communicate more effectively, and better utilize capital resources. Without all the bureaucratic delays and competing agendas, we saw immediate improvements in Guest satisfaction scores and Cast attitudes. We also saw dramatically lower costs. For instance, because the purchasing system was consolidated, every department now used the same ingredients and raw materials, saving the company millions of dollars in volume discounts. Plus we now felt like one strong, cohesive team working together for a common purpose. As a result, we were better positioned to react to unexpected events with speed, clarity, and precision.

The point is, structure is as important to an organization as it is to a building. No matter what industry you're in, one of your challenges as a leader is to evaluate the structure on an ongoing basis and not to be afraid to break the mold. Remember, a great leader never settles for good enough. Here are some practical strategies to guide your way.

1. Be clear about who's responsible for what. Every individual in your organization should clearly and completely understand what he or she is responsible for, what level of authority he or she has, and how he or she will be held accountable. Each employee also needs to know what *others* are responsible for, what authority *others* have, and how *others* will be held accountable. Without clarity on those points, confusion and mishaps are inevitable.

When the lines of authority in Disney's food and beverage operation were unclear, inconsistent decisions were constantly being made. For example, because we did not have one central executive responsible for pricing, the price of similar items varied widely throughout Walt Disney World. So a child's meal might cost $2.99 in one restaurant and $5.99 in another, or the same size Coke might be $1.39 at a concession stand in one of the parks and $2.99 at a resort snack bar. And because no one had the final say on purchasing, chefs were allowed to order according to their individual preferences—not a good structure for a billion-dollar food enterprise. At times we were purchasing as many as 25 kinds of french fries and 130 different pastas, resulting in higher prices from vendors because they had to warehouse so many similar products.

To fix the situation, I brought in an outside consultant from Chicago, Glen Wolfson, who spent three intense days with me and a group of managers. We listed fifty-eight typical decisions that had to be made on a regular basis, then talked them through until we settled on one person or position to have the final responsibility for each. The pricing decisions for all services and products, for example, would now be made by a centralized group with an overall view of the entire operation, and the purchasing department would have final authority on food orders—after working with the chefs to identify the best products.

The improvements were immediate, with no loss of quality for our Guests. Because everyone knew exactly what he or she was responsible for, operations ran much more smoothly and cleanly. Teamwork improved dramatically, and arguments over authority virtually disappeared. As for the bottom line, reducing the variety of fries alone resulted in a half-million-dollar savings, and our overall costs dropped steadily year after year.

Clear communication is one of a leader's principal tasks, especially when it comes to responsibility and authority. Keep that concept in mind at all times, and your teams will perform above expectations.

2. Remember that responsibility and authority go hand in hand. If you give people responsibility without also giving them the necessary authority to carry out those responsibilities, you are setting them up for failure. If you tell someone, "It's up to you to get this done," but you don't also say, "You are empowered to make whatever decisions are necessary to do it," and

"You'll have all the resources you need," you are giving that person responsibility without authority. That can be an untenable position—and, by the way, one of the leading causes of stress.

Because I was head of operations, Al Weiss held me responsible for Guest satisfaction at Walt Disney World. In that context, I delegated responsibility and authority to various people: Most food and beverage decisions went to Dieter Hannig, most decisions about maintenance to Jeff Vahle, and most decisions for daily resort operations to Erin Wallace and Karl Holz. But while they had complete authority to make these decisions, in the end I was the only one responsible for the outcomes. So I made clear agreements with each of them about when I needed to be involved in decisions and when I did not, and I established routine procedures for communicating with them. This allowed them to assume high levels of day-to-day responsibility and authority while I retained ultimate responsibility for the end results. Excellent communication and trust were the keys to this sharing of responsibility and authority.

That's the key point: As a leader you are *always* responsible for the outcome. Too often in business, a leader's response to things gone wrong is: "Why wasn't I informed?" or "I delegated that responsibility to Jim." The fact is, if things go wrong, it's the leader's responsibility. So make sure everyone knows exactly what outcomes you expect and exactly what authority he or she has and doesn't have, and install rigorous procedures for keeping informed. At the end of the day there should be no confusion about who is authorized to take which actions and what the results of those actions should be.

3. Make every position count. Making sure that every position has genuine value can be difficult, but it's a challenge that leaders have to face squarely. Ask yourself these questions:

✳ Does this position create real value for our company?

✳ What would happen if we eliminated this position?

✳ What would happen if we redistributed this position's direct reports to others who can handle more responsibility?

✳ What would happen if this were a part-time position?

✳ What would happen if we outsourced this position's responsibilities?

✳ What would happen if we changed our structure or processes so we no longer needed this position?

✳ What would happen if we automated this position so it became self-service, the way ATMs are for banks and Web sites are for booking travel?

Let's face it, answering these questions can force you to make emotionally wrenching decisions. No leader wants to let go of a longtime employee who no longer fits or to move someone to a less responsible role and risk making him or her feel demoted. But leaders can't let anyone "hide" within the organization, and that means analyzing the value of every position objectively. Don't fall into traps such as giving long-time employees whose positions are no longer essential new titles with no real responsibility. You're not doing them a favor. If you determine that a position has become superfluous, you have to find a way to balance the bottom line with your concern for that person's well-being.

My first choice was always to reassign people whose jobs had to be eliminated, and at Disney I was successful in doing that 90 percent of the time. But there are times when it's simply not possible. Once, for instance, I decided to eliminate a certain high-level executive position that reported to me. It was an extremely difficult decision because the person in that role was an outstanding leader whom I hated to lose. But it was the right business decision; it was clear that the people who reported to him could perform much more efficiently if they reported directly to me. Plus the company would save his six-figure salary and the cost of his support staff. So I met with the executive personally and told him immediately that his position was being eliminated because we were reorganizing our whole retail business in both food and beverage and merchandise. I said that his support staff would be reassigned but that there was no suitable position available for someone of his expertise and experience. He was of course shocked and upset. Still, I did everything in my power to soften the blow and make sure the story had a happy ending. I gave him several months to find a new job and told him to make it his highest priority and to take as much time off as necessary to update his résumé, make phone calls, and go to interviews. I also offered to serve as a reference and put him in touch with other companies as well as executive search firms with which I had strong relationships. In the end it worked out fine for both him and Disney. He began a satisfying new career as a consultant and served on several corporate boards.

Obviously, in a large corporation with steady growth and plenty of opportunities for internal mobility, it's easier to make structural changes without causing too much hardship. I realize that not every leader has that luxury. In the event that you do have to let go of valued employees, I urge you to approach these difficult situations in a humane manner. Communicate quickly, directly, and honestly with the person involved. Explain exactly why the position is being eliminated, give the person as much time as possible to find another job, either inside or outside the company, and offer to write a recommendation. When you are forced to let decent people go, treat them the way you would want to be treated in that situation: with dignity. Not only is this the ethical thing to do, but it also sends the right message to the rest of the organization. In my experience, going the extra mile to ease someone's departure and make the transition easier always pays off, not only in the person's gratitude but also in the trust and loyalty of the rest of the workforce.

4. Get as flat as you can. It is almost always a good idea to minimize the number of layers in your organization, so you can deal directly with as many people as possible. Each layer through which information is filtered multiplies the inaccuracies and distortions, making it much more likely that something minor will snowball into a serious problem. If you've ever played the children's game telephone, in which a sentence is whispered from one person to another in a circle, you know what I mean. It's amazing how different the message is by the time it completes the round.

In addition to clearing up the channels of communication, there are other advantages to having as many people as possible report directly to you. One is that it forces you to get really good at delegating. Another is that it encourages you to hire the absolute best direct reports. I'll discuss hiring in the next chapter, but in this context the key factor is this: The better your direct reports, the *more* of them you can have. Why? Because they need very little supervision. Mediocre people take up more of your time because you constantly have to help them, coach them, and put out their fires. You become more of a hand holder than a leader. There were times at Walt Disney

World when I had as many as fourteen executives reporting to me and other times when I had as few as six. Invariably, the more direct reports I had, the better the organization functioned. That was because the executives I hired were so good I could get out of their way once we identified our desired outcomes. Another advantage is that with a flat structure you have fewer total salaries (fewer managers and executives also mean fewer assistants, secretaries, and other support staff), which means you can afford to hire top-notch people and pay them better.

Overall, a flat structure enhances productivity by streamlining the decision-making process, speeding up follow-through, and optimizing communication. Fewer layers mean fewer mistakes, misunderstandings, mistranslations, and other misses.

Bear in mind that flattening doesn't apply only to the top rungs of an organization, nor does it necessarily mean eliminating jobs. Sometimes a small shift at a lower level can yield big results. For example, several years ago the shipping department in Disney World's Textile Services was having problems dealing with service calls from fellow Cast Members. A resort manager might phone the laundry in a panic because the pool was swarming with kids and he or she needed more towels. A restaurant manager might call because the tablecloths he or she had ordered had never arrived and the manager was expecting a big dinner crowd. The Textile Services manager who took the call would then tell the shipping department to take care of the situation. But these managers were busy people, so some of the orders fell through the cracks. Fortunately, one manager who had great confidence in Cast Members had an idea: Let's eliminate the middleman. Since the shipping system operators were ideally situated to take care of problems on the spot, why not train some of them to take service calls directly? For their added responsibility, the operators selected were bumped up to coordinator pay—an extra fifty cents an hour for them and not a large expense for Disney. The payoff was terrific. Not only did the new system free up the managers in Textile Services from having to deal with crises, but it enhanced the sense of pride and ownership among the Cast Members in the shipping department and improved the speed and efficiency with which calls were handled.

5. Eliminate overwork. Needless to say, there are exceptions to every rule. If your employees are feeling overworked, it can sometimes make sense to *add* a layer. Ask yourself: "Do people in your organization complain about being overwhelmed? Do they mumble about not having time to do everything that's asked of them?" This happens at times in most companies, and Walt Disney World is no exception. We were pushing managers to be personally involved with the leadership development of their direct reports while spending up to 80 percent of their day on the front lines with Guests and Cast Members. But there simply weren't enough hours in the day for them to do it all. We responded by cutting other expenses and using the savings to create new administrative positions called coordinators. The coordinators took over some of the managers' routine responsibilities so they had time to train and develop their teams and deal directly with Guests.

If you get wind of grievances about overwork, the culprit might be the organizational structure. Ask yourself these questions, which apply to every type of organization.

✳ Is the overall structure getting in the way of productivity?

* Are departments or teams disorganized? Could they be organized in a better way?

* Are employees spending time on work that no longer has the value it once did?

* Can certain tasks be streamlined or even eliminated?

* Would employees work more efficiently if they were given more authority?

* Do employees need training in time management?

Reworking your organizational design might lighten your employees' workload and make every hour of their time more productive. Simply reviewing the tasks everyone is doing and eliminating those of lesser value can be a major step in that direction. Also, if you eliminate positions that have become superfluous, you can use some of the money you save to bring on additional administrative help or to automate certain functions. Finally, consider giving more authority to trusted front-line managers. It can free them to make decisions quickly without the endless reports and meetings needed to get approval from those higher up in the organization.

6. Rethink the meeting structure. One typical symptom of a flawed organizational design is too much time spent in meetings. If your employees complain about useless meetings or meetings that last too long, you may want to rethink the contents of the meetings, how often they are being held, and who is being included.

The first step is to identify the goals of your meetings. Then evaluate whether those goals are being served by the current structure. One productive meeting a month can be more valuable than one poorly planned meeting a week. I learned that lesson when some of my direct reports read me the riot act. They said our weekly meetings were wasteful because we spent too much time discussing things of low importance just to fill up the time allotted. They suggested we hold them once a month instead. I went along with their recommendation, and was I ever glad! Our new monthly gatherings were jam-packed with important, productive work, without a minute wasted. The agendas were limited to important items, and lesser issues were easily handled by e-mail, telephone, and impromptu one-on-one conversations. If an important matter came up unexpectedly, we simply called a special meeting to deal with it.

The incident taught me that the best way to evaluate the effectiveness of meetings is to get honest feedback from the people who attend them. Ask if the meetings are held too often or not often enough. Ask if they drag on too long or are too rushed. Also ask if the right people are included. Once you've identified the problems, invite key people to think up ways to make the meetings more useful, more productive, and more enjoyable, so that everyone who attends receives good value for the time spent. In my experience, the better prepared the leader is, the more efficient and effective the meeting will be. Ideally, you should prepare your agenda well ahead of time and send it out forty-eight hours in advance to give the attendees plenty of time to prepare. Then use that agenda to keep the meeting on track and on time. Also, while I'm speaking of time, every meeting should begin on time whether everyone is there or not and should end at the set time. Word will get out soon enough, and the bad habit of showing up late will quickly change.

Another key is to invite only those people who *need* to attend. Essentially, there are two types of meeting, and knowing the difference will help you determine who should be included. The basic purpose of one type is to give out information; the purpose of the other is to solve problems. If you're holding a meeting to give out information, you should include everyone on your team or in your department, so no one is left in the dark. If your meeting is designed to solve a particular problem, include only those directly affected by it. If you have ever been in a meeting where the group starts to address a specific problem and you wonder why in the world you're there—and almost everyone in business has at one point or another—then your leader did not clearly understand the difference between the two types of meeting.

A great many meetings are held just so the boss can keep in touch with his employees, a worthy intention, but one that can be accomplished in more effective ways, like having one-on-one conversations and visiting with people in their workplace. Great leaders keep in constant touch with employees, but they gather them together only when it's truly necessary. So, have an open discussion with your team about how to schedule and structure meetings for maximum efficiency and effectiveness. I guarantee you that the people who attend them will appreciate the effort.

7. *Anyone can take responsibility for change.* By now you might be thinking, "This is all well and good, but evaluating the organizational structure is not in my job description. Not only that, I don't have the responsibility or the authority to make structural changes." Wrong! You don't have to be officially in charge to influence organizational structure. If you have ideas for doing things better, write them up and present them to the person you report to. But don't come across as a complainer.

Deliver your proposal in a professional manner, and focus on the relevant positions and responsibilities, not on the people who do them.

By the same token, if you do have the authority to make these kinds of changes, make sure every employee knows that his or her input is welcome. At Disney I always told Cast Members, "Part of your salary is for giving us your opinions." Everyone was encouraged and empowered to evaluate the structure on an ongoing basis and to submit recommendations in writing. Remember, people on the front lines see things you don't, like who doesn't have enough responsibility and who is being stretched too thin and where communication is breaking down because of structural flaws.

Once, when I was walking through one of the Disney World resorts, a frontline Cast Member approached me and suggested that we re-evaluate the positions we called leads. Those jobs had been created in 1971 to give frontline Cast Members with technical expertise the opportunity to train new hires. Over the years the positions had evolved to include some managerial responsibilities, even though the leads had no formal management training. While many of them did perfectly good jobs, this Cast Member told me, others were abusing their positions by showing favoritism in scheduling days off, and some were even disciplining fellow Cast Members—*not* in their job description.

The Cast Member's suggestion made a lot of sense to me. In fact, I had thought of doing away with the position entirely, because we had successfully opened our Paris operation without any leads. But I hesitated because there were hundreds of leads at Walt Disney World, and eliminating their positions was bound to cause some pain. Plus, leads were such fixtures that most Disney managers could not imagine operating without them. Moreover, since I had not been in Orlando very long at the time, I didn't think it would be a good idea to make waves yet. But after hearing that Cast Member's perspective, I shared the idea with my team and my boss, and we formulated a plan to put some of the leads into a management training program and transfer the others back to frontline positions. Once I was sure that no jobs would be lost, I had the confidence to pursue the objective. Even though we later added new hourly positions to help with technical training, the change saved millions of dollars in labor costs, and many of the leads went on to become some of our best managers. And it would never have happened if not for the initiative of one Cast Member. That's the value of having a culture in which the free flow of ideas is common practice.

8. Be prepared to take risks. It has been said that two attitudes toward change can sabotage success. One is: "But this is the way we've always done it." The other is: "But we've never done it that way before." Don't fall prey to either of these. Always look for a better way to do things, and don't be afraid of upsetting people. If you have a good idea, give it a chance. Remember, if it doesn't work out, you can always change it again.

There are only two kinds of decisions in life: those that are reversible and those that aren't. If you're on the fence about making a structural change, ask yourself this question: "Is the decision reversible or nonreversible?" Doing this has helped give me the confidence to take risks; I lean toward saying yes to risks when the decision is reversible and am more careful, exercising all due diligence, when it is not. The story that opens this chapter is a good example. Because the decision to have chefs report directly to GMs could have been reversed, it was easier to give the idea a go. Ditto for getting rid of the leads position.

The reversible-irreversible test has enabled me to say yes more often than no when people make suggestions, and leaders who always say no find that their teams stop coming to them with fresh ideas. So remember, there's no shame in reversing a decision that isn't working out the way you planned. It's all part of the healthy process of change.

9. Expect resistance. Whenever you suggest major structural changes, some people in the organization will invariably fight it. Some folks are simply uncomfortable with change and cling to the status quo. Others fear that when the dust settles, they'll be among the casualties. Great leaders listen to those objections seriously and pay attention to reasonable arguments. But when they think they're on the right track, they don't let the resistance of others stop them from doing what they believe in. It's vital therefore to anticipate resistance, accept it, and honor it, but if you've done due diligence and you're sure you're on the right course, don't be afraid to stick to your convictions.

One structural change that met with resistance at Disney World was our decision to save money by hiring an outside company to clean certain areas of the hotels. To minimize the impact, we outsourced only the nighttime cleaning, and we made a commitment to reassign Cast Members whose jobs were affected. Still, there was resistance from union representatives and some of our managers. We treated those who disagreed respectfully, but we stayed on track. The key to overcoming the resistance was our sincerity about preserving every Cast Member's job and salary. Some had to give up the pay differential for working the night shift, but there was enough overtime available for those who needed extra money to make up for it. A few people were unhappy with their new shifts, but they adjusted over time, and in the end it worked out just fine for everyone. Our properties were as clean as ever, and we reduced our costs significantly.

You can expect resistance to structural change even in the tiniest organization. Remember Laurie Kotas, the CEO of Wishland, whom you met in Chapter Three? As her nonprofit grew, she felt the need to have each staff member focus on one area instead of keeping his or her hand in everything, as is typical in small operations. Predictably, people thought that something was being taken away from them, instead of their being freed up to do one thing even better. "In the past," says Laurie, "I'd be overwhelmed by the thought of losing someone who couldn't change. It would upset me emotionally." After learning about the importance of structural change at the Disney Institute, she was able to stick to her convictions and work hard to get buy-in from the resisters. She also learned that it's sometimes necessary to make the tough choice to let a good person go.

Because people naturally resist change, great leaders orient their people not only to expect change but to *welcome* it. In fact, they take it a step further: They train people to look for positive ways to *initiate* change. One tactic for doing so came to me spontaneously in 1994, and it has since become a personal trademark.

We were preparing to announce organizational changes that would do away with some traditional positions in hotel management. Because it was somewhat drastic, I knew the policy would be met with stiff resistance, so I decided to give a speech on the topic of change to a few hundred members of the management team. I needed to reach both their hearts and minds with this message: It is time for us, as leaders, to step up and try new ways to structure our organization. I knew if I got it right, it would set the stage for the positive transformation of the company. But while working on the script, I hit a dead end. I just couldn't think of a powerful way to convince managers that breaking the mold was necessary.

Frustrated, I went home that night looking forward to my favorite meal, Priscilla's magnificent meat loaf, with mashed potatoes, fresh brussels sprouts, and a generous splash of Tabasco sauce to spice things up a little. A family tradition for twenty-five years, the meal was guaranteed to raise my spirits. But when I sat down at the table, I immediately saw that something had changed. The Tabasco sauce was there all right, but it wasn't red. It was *green*. I had never even heard of green Tabasco sauce. I wanted good old trusty *red* Tabasco sauce. But Priscilla thought we should give it a try. I didn't want to, but she held firm, so I put a couple of drops of the weird-looking stuff on a corner of my meat loaf and took a bite. And guess what? It was fantastic. A phrase flashed in my head like a neon sign: "People like change until it shows up at their doorstep." Now I knew exactly what I would say in the most important speech of my career.

When the time came, I stepped to the microphone and slammed two bottles of Tabasco sauce, one red and one green, onto the podium. I said, "Can you imagine the reaction at that company when someone suggested they produce green Tabasco? Red Tabasco had been the *only* Tabasco for over one hundred and twenty-five years." I then told the audience how I'd resisted the green variety myself, only to become a faithful convert thanks to Priscilla's determination. Now, I added, we use both colors in our house. And we weren't the only ones; the company was selling an awful lot of both kinds.

A few months later I introduced the Green Tabasco Award, which I presented to leaders who demonstrated the courage to try new ways of doing things. I simply wrote each name on a bottle of green Tabasco sauce and presented it with some comments about how his or her innovation had improved our business. The award became a symbol of positive change. You might want to do something of your own along the same lines.

The moral of the story is this: People don't always recognize the merits of change right off the bat. But if you persist, they'll soon come to see why breaking the mold is not only in the best interest of the company but in their best interest as well, and they may even follow your example by initiating changes themselves.

10. Don't try to win every battle. This is a caveat for the previous point. While leaders need to be persistent and determined in the face of resistance, they also have to be flexible enough to fine-tune their vision at every step. The resisters might have very good reasons for opposing your plan, so listen to them carefully. You can't fall on your sword for every issue, so it's crucial to know when to let go and save your energy to fight another day. Ask yourself whether you're fighting for a truly worthwhile goal or because you can't admit you were wrong or you have to win, no matter what. Nobody likes to work for leaders who use their positions to go after personal victories at the expense of the organization's long-term health.

I have worked with many leaders who were too competitive for their own good. When I worked at Marriott, the company brought in some executives from another famous hotel chain to shake things up. Well, they shook things up all right. They were so intent on establishing their power that they didn't bother to get to know the operations and the people before they started making wholesale changes. They changed the restaurant concepts without much thought or consultation (the move was quickly reversed because customers complained directly to Bill Marriott's office). They pushed out competent managers and replaced them with former colleagues of theirs whose authoritarian ways did not fit the Marriott culture. Sure, they were smart, experienced, and technically proficient. But they treated people with disrespect. They made decisions without consultation and dismissed questions and suggestions with disdain, because they were right and that was all there was to it. They were so belligerent that the frightened employees avoided them as best they could. They had come to Marriott believing they could quickly implement their old companies' ways of doing things. But by abusing their authority, they piled up personal victories at the cost of morale, commitment, and teamwork. After a rough eighteen months they finally left the company. Once superstars in the industry, most of them have since had lackluster careers, bouncing from one position to another and one company to another.

So don't confuse being persuasive with winning at all costs. If you trust your vision, by all means work to overcome the resistance and stick to your guns. The results will speak for themselves. But if the resisters offer compelling arguments and solid evidence, don't be too stubborn to back down. People respect leaders who pick their battles and can admit to being wrong every once in a while.

11. You're never really done. Once you have a great structure in place, don't rest on your laurels. No matter how good you think your design is or how proud you are of it, stand prepared to change it again if the circumstances demand it.

Remember, the changes you initiate might seem forward-leaning today, but they will be tradition tomorrow. The innovative structure you put into place one year will be "the way things are" the next. In fact, to the newer people in your organization, they will be "the way it's always been." If you don't continuously re-evaluate your structure, you run the risk of becoming the old-timer who resists change. And the moment you do, someone with a fresh perspective will be ready to replace you—especially in this day and age, when technology constantly forces us to adjust the way work is performed and managed. Imagine a travel agency that stubbornly kept booking trips by telephone after automated systems came along or an executive who refused to learn how to use a computer because "that's secretary's work."

It's not always obvious when a structural change is called for, especially when business is good. However, if you don't question the status quo, you'll be forced to change under pressure once it's obvious that your structure is no longer working. So look for signs like these: People complain about red tape; jokes about company bureaucrats become commonplace; employees say they feel like drones or robots; go-getters feel underused or say their jobs are not challenging; leaders feel frustrated because they don't have the authority to fulfill their responsibilities; creative people are leaving the company. If you see such signs, you should consider retooling the structure. But don't wait for trouble. Sometimes the best ideas come when things are rolling along just fine and you need to take the next leap forward.

Here is a delicious irony: The better your organizational structure, the easier it is to change it. Why? Because an excellent structure has built-in adaptability. If you have created a culture of change, in which everyone from top to bottom is empowered to find creative ways to improve the organization, you'll be better able to adjust to unexpected events and emergencies. I learned that lesson firsthand at World Disney World. Being in Florida, we always had to be prepared for hurricanes, so we had a structure in place for responding to emergencies. As a result, on 9/11, once we received word about the horrible events that were unfolding, all relevant personnel knew exactly where to go and what to do, and we were able to make key decisions within half an hour: to mobilize buses and evacuate the fifty thousand people in the theme parks; to provide free hotel rooms to everyone who was stranded; to give cash and food vouchers to any Guest who needed money to eat; to suspend charges for phone calls to anywhere in the world; and to send costumed entertainers to occupy the frightened children.

Once the chaos subsided and the park reopened, we faced new challenges because of the drastic decline in revenues and the uncertain future of tourism. We knew we'd have to make structural changes quickly. The first decision was made by Al Weiss: We would not lay off a single person. We had to find other ways to cut costs. So we closed a few attractions and a thousand-room resort, and maximized manpower by having Cast Members rotate through multiple locations. We froze wages and hiring temporarily, reduced working hours, and strongly encouraged Cast Members to use up their accrued vacation time. Combined with other cost-cutting ideas (you'll read about some in later chapters), these structural moves enabled us to keep everyone employed and all the operations running until revenues returned to their former levels. By that Christmas everyone in our Cast was able to work full-time once again. While there was short-term pain for all, we ended up with an even stronger organizational structure that could stand up to the toughest of circumstances.

We didn't stop there. We kept looking for more efficient ways to organize. For example, we soon gave several general managers two resort hotels to manage instead of one. By doubling the size of the manager's team, we could move custodial workers or kitchen staff back and forth between operations, leading to an immediate boost in productivity and a drastic improvement in Guest service.

The leaders I helped train continue to carry on the culture of creative change. As I write this, Disney Parks and Resorts is going through major changes in organizational structure. For the last two years it has been moving toward a more centralized approach, with executives having worldwide responsibility for areas such as food and beverage, merchandise, attractions, and maintenance in order to capture the best practices from all the company's operations and implement them quickly around the world.

ACTION STEPS

Use these two checklists to evaluate whether the structure of your organization is working well or it might be time for a change.

The current structure is successful if:

√ The operation runs fluidly in your absence.

√ The lines of accountability, responsibility, and authority are clear.

√ Decisions are made easily and efficiently.

√ Information flows to all levels smoothly.

√ Answers get to the right people quickly.

The current structure is not working if:

√ People complain about wasted time, unclear roles, and miscommunication.

√ Too many people get involved in every decision.

√ Ineffective workers "hide" within the system.

√ There are too many or too few direct reports per manager.

√ Meetings are overly long, too frequent, or unproductive.

CHAPTER FIVE

STRATEGY #3

MAKE YOUR PEOPLE
YOUR BRAND

G reat food is an important part of the overall Disney experience. During my tenure at *Walt Disney World®* Resort, the cuisine went from mediocre to excellent, earning accolades from Guests and food critics alike. One day I joked with my boss, Al Weiss, that I deserved all the credit because I was the one who had hired Dieter Hannig and made him director of food and beverage (and later senior vice president). A professionally trained chef who knows the business inside and out, Dieter has technical expertise that is matched by consummate professionalism, impeccable people skills, and a gift for conjuring delicious meals out of fresh, healthy ingredients. He is the single biggest reason for the excellent reputation of Disney World's restaurants, from quick service to elegant table dining.

Early in my career I thought that a strong brand was the most important thing an organization could have. Many people think of a brand in terms of a product or a logo, but I soon discovered that in reality, your *people* are your brand. No matter how good your products and services are, you can't achieve true excellence unless you attract great people, develop great people, and keep great people. Once I learned how to do this, my life as an executive became a whole lot easier because I was blessed with direct reports who were as pleasant as they were competent. Everyone on the team had total respect for everyone else, both as professionals and as individuals, and I never had to worry about our ability to implement a decision, no matter how challenging the situation may have seemed.

Like practicing good preventive medicine, hiring and promoting the right people will spare you a lot of painful and costly problems. The suggestions that follow take time and effort, but they will give you a competitive advantage that can't be easily imitated.

1. Define the perfect candidate. When you recruit or hire someone, it's vital to be totally clear on what you're looking for. Exactly what qualities do you want in the person you hire? What sort of skills do you expect him or her to have? What do you want him or her to be able to accomplish? Such questions should be contemplated carefully and thoroughly by everyone involved in the decision. You may not always find *the* perfect person, but you will surely get a better one if you aim for the ideal.

Regardless of the position you're hiring for, I recommend evaluating candidates according to the following four areas of competency:

> ✳ *Technical competence.* This simply means having the requisite knowledge and skills to do the job. Accountants need

to understand tax laws and have the financial acumen to manage the books; the folks who make deliveries should know how to drive the trucks; a chef has to have great recipes and know how to assemble the proper ingredients to put together delicious meals.

* *Management competence.* Every employee should be disciplined, self-controlled, and organized. An investment banker with dozens of clients needs to be on top of trades and investment portfolios; a buyer at a shoe store needs to be able to keep track of inventory, orders, and returns; and a caterer who turns out a hundred or a thousand meals every night has to organize supplies, keep expenses in line, and juggle various menus. No matter what position I was hiring for, I always looked for people who had a system for planning their days. I often say that my best friend is my Day-Timer. We've been together more than twenty-five years, and I call it my backup brain. Whenever I can't find my Day-Timer for a few minutes, I get that sickening feeling in my stomach that parents get when they think they've lost their children. I have a BlackBerry too! It is my *next* best friend. So when you're evaluating a potential hire, make sure he or she has an effective organizational system.

* *Technological competence.* Everyone needs to understand and utilize available technologies relevant to his or her position. A nurse, for instance, has to know what instruments, software, and machines to use to manage injections or measure heart rate; a car mechanic needs to know what gadgets and tools to use to fix an engine; a server at the drive-through lane at McDonald's needs to know how to operate the system that sends an order

straight to a screen in the kitchen. And the decision makers at the hospital, the repair shop, and the fast-food company need to know about cutting-edge technologies to stay ahead of the curve, and they always need to be looking for the next technological advancement that can improve results.

✳ *Leadership competence.* Since this entire book is about leadership, nothing needs to be said here except this: The ability to lead is something to look for in everyone you consider hiring, no matter what the position is. A head chef may be a great culinary artist, but if he or she does not hire the right people, train them well, and inspire them to prepare every single dish perfectly, he or she will quickly end up cooking for one.

2. Don't settle for a clone. When filling a position, don't look for a replica of the person who's leaving; different times often call for different skills and experience, even if the job title remains the same. For instance, at a time when your company has a lot of new employees, you might need a manager who's great at training; at another time, when profit margins are sagging, you might want to fill that position with someone with strong financial skills. Evaluate the business climate, as well as your existing team, to see what talents are most needed *now,* and focus on finding someone who can supply them. Every job opening is an opportunity to redefine the role.

At Walt Disney World we once needed someone to replace the head of the call center, who was responsible for more than two thousand agents. George Kalogridis, who was the VP for operations at Epcot at the time, was our choice for the job, even though he had no prior experience in anything resembling a call center. When his predecessor had been hired, we had looked for someone with a call center background and extensive technical knowledge. Now those qualities were less important; we needed a great leader. Our call centers were plagued with high Cast turnover and difficulties with training procedures, and George's proven knack for attracting people with expertise and inspiring them to do excellent work was just what the doctor ordered. Before long the operation enjoyed a complete turnaround: Cast turnover dropped dramatically, and productivity and Guest satisfaction went way up.

3. Look for good people in unlikely places. Sometimes you can find the best hires in the places you least expect to. Hiring George for that call center position meant having to find someone to replace him as VP of operations at Epcot. Again, my choice was an unlikely candidate. Brad Rex, our VP of labor management, had zero experience with Disney operations. A graduate of the U.S. Naval Academy and Harvard Business School, he'd served as an officer on a nuclear submarine and worked for British Petroleum before coming to Disney to work in financial planning. When I tapped him to run Epcot's operations, the entire organization was surprised. But I liked Brad's business background, his problem-solving and critical thinking skills, and his demonstrated talent for inspiring and leading teams. We familiarized him with the technical aspects of park operations through a cross-training program and then turned him loose. Over the next five years he led Epcot to new highs in Cast satisfaction, Guest satisfaction, and business results. And in the difficult period after 9/11, Brad's background in finance and labor management helped us control costs and keep the Cast focused on great Guest service.

So don't just look in the obvious places, and don't reject

candidates out of hand simply because they don't square with the standard profile for that job. If they have the competency to perform well and the leadership ability to inspire others, don't hold their unconventional backgrounds against them. In fact, you never know what gifts they might be bringing with them, as one of my favorite Disney World stories illustrates.

In the flatworks department of Textile Services, the Cast Members are expected to run a certain number of pieces through the ironing machine every hour. They feed the sheets and pillowcases onto a wide conveyor belt and keep them in a straight line as they ride under and over three large metal rollers, then out the back of the machine, where each piece is folded by a compressed-air device. A long loop of ironer tape runs through the machinery, to guide the linen through the rollers in a smooth and orderly way. The tape loop is continuous, but the total length is made up of several pieces that are tied together in knots. Sometimes those knots broke, the machines jammed, and the frustrated Cast Members had to stop everything and fix the knot. And they were being held accountable for the number of pieces that completed the process.

At one point a craft maintenance engineer (the lowest-level engineer on staff) named J. R. Garcia approached the leadership team and offered to change the knot so it would hold together better. He tried some different kinds of knots and soon found one that worked. It's still being used, and Ken Miratsky, the manager of the housekeeping laundry, says it has saved the company about forty thousand dollars a year in tape; that's more than half a million dollars since it was introduced thirteen years ago. How did J.R. know about knots? It wasn't part of his Disney World training, but it *was* part of the training he'd received in the navy, where he'd served on a submarine. J.R. became a foreman, moved up to manager, then to head engineer for all three laundries, and now he's the director of Textile Services.

4. Involve the team in the selection process. How many times have you been shocked by an announcement about a new hire? Have you ever wondered why no one consulted with you before so-and-so was promoted to a certain position? It's amazing how often executives make such vital decisions without involving the rest of the team.

Great leaders go beyond human resources and search firms; they give selected team members the chance to evaluate or interview the candidates. Think that's a waste of time? Think again. Other people on your team might ask the candidates questions you haven't thought of. Their conversations will veer in different directions and draw out different information. When everyone is finished, you'll have a more complete portrait of the candidates. Also, since everyone on your team will have to work with the new hire, you'll have a better chance of choosing a good fit. Not only that, but the transition will be smoother because the person being hired will be familiar with the team.

At Disney we implemented a system for letting certain frontline Cast Members interview candidates for managerial positions. The policy was consistent with our vision that leaders should serve their subordinates, not the other way around, and it quickly proved useful. The Cast asked sharp, pointed questions, not only about obvious issues like scheduling and training, but important concerns like how closely the candidates intended to work with Cast Members, how available they would be, and whom they'd involve in making decisions. Some managers called these the toughest and most thoughtful interviews they'd ever been through. Of course the frontline Cast Members did not have the final say; their report was combined with the candidate's leadership profile and interviews conducted by management, and the whole package would be sent to the leader responsible for the final decision. But the Cast's input was considered a crucial piece of the puzzle and was often the deciding factor.

This strategy of involving a wide range of employees in the hiring process has been adopted with great success by numerous organizations in a wide variety of industries. One example is Michigan-based Guardian Industries, one of the world's largest manufacturers of glass products, with more than one hundred plants worldwide and about twenty thousand employees. After the company's managers attended a Disney Institute training course, they decided to include hourly workers in the interview process. They started to train selected people to do interviewing, in addition to the relevant manager and department head, and those same employees were encouraged to serve as role models and trainers for the new hires. Now, they said, they have "a more robust system for hiring and training." There is no reason your organization, whatever its purpose and whatever its size, can't do the same.

5. Select by talent, not by résumé. When you read a résumé, always keep in mind who wrote it. An estimated 40 percent of résumés are said to contain exaggerations in such areas as educational background and previous job titles, responsibilities, and accomplishments. Think of them as advertisements, not objective reports.

When I worked at Marriott, I once interviewed a man for a chef's position. His résumé said he had worked as a cook for the state of Pennsylvania. Turns out it wasn't a total fabrication: He had done time in a state prison, where he'd worked in the kitchen. I didn't hire him—not because he'd been in prison (I'd hired ex-convicts before, and they hadn't let me down) but because he hadn't told the whole truth. I knew I would not be able to trust him once he was on the job.

Another time, at Walt Disney World, I rejected a candidate for director of merchandise because his résumé said he had a college degree, which turned out not to be so. I would have hired him *without* the degree because he had excellent experience and the right set of talents. But not only had he fabricated his education, he had also tried to cover up his lie. When we told him that our background check could not verify that he'd received a degree, instead of owning up, he claimed it was a clerical error.

So read résumés with a skeptical eye, and don't take falsifications and exaggerations lightly. Deceptiveness is usually a far worse sign than whatever shortcoming a candidate is trying to cover up.

6. Find a good fit. Once, at Disney World, we hired an excellent chef for one of our best restaurants even though he had a reputation for not treating people well. He was said to be an autocratic egomaniac who was difficult to work with. But we were so dazzled by his artistry and technical skills that we talked ourselves into believing we could transform him. We quickly learned that even Disney magic can't change the spots on every leopard. Even though we had explained the leadership style we expected of managers before we hired him, he verbally abused Cast Members and treated them disrespectfully. He lasted less than ninety days before he was fired.

After that experience I vowed to consider "team chemistry"

in every hiring decision I made. In trying to match the candidate's personality with the organizational culture, I turned away many qualified people because they did not have the relationship skills or political sensitivity for a particular environment. My colleagues and I knew that managers and executives who liked being Lone Rangers would not go over well in Disney's team-oriented culture. Candidates who seemed to need to be totally in charge at all times or were not capable of sharing power were simply not hired, no matter how gifted they were or how much experience they had.

We used several methods to determine whether potential leaders would blend in. First and foremost, we tried to promote from within the company, so we were familiar with the person's work style and personality traits. When reaching outside the company, we made multiple reference checks in an effort to understand the candidates as well as we could. The Cast Members' interviews helped us judge whether or not someone would fit in with an established team. For high-level management positions, we had the Gallup Organization produce detailed leadership profiles of the candidates (see number 11), and we spent a lot of time with them to make sure they clearly understood our expectations. With potential executives, I personally took at least four hours to go over the Disney Great Leader Strategies line by line, watching their reactions at every step.

Bottom line: Your organization's culture is the product of the people in it, and every addition and subtraction will alter the chemistry. Do everything you can to keep it harmonious.

7. *Hire people who are smarter and more talented than you.* No matter how smart or talented you are, there will always be someone who is better than you in at least one important aspect of your work. Insecure leaders run from these people; great leaders seek them out.

Let's face it, being in the presence of exceptional talent can be profoundly inspiring, but it can also arouse feelings of resentment and envy. Great leaders don't let personal insecurities get in the way of success. Rather than be afraid to be outshone by a subordinate with exceptional talent, they're proud to be known for recognizing and hiring outstanding talent. I know I owe much of my success to the fact that virtually every person who worked for me was a whole lot better at certain things than I was. My team at Disney World—Erin Wallace, Chris Bostick, Alice Norsworthy, Bud Dare, Jeff Vahle, Dieter Hannig, Liz Boice, Joan Ryan, Greg Emmer, Rich Taylor, Karl Holz, and Don Robinson, to name just a few—were true experts in their areas of responsibility. I'm proud that many of them went on to bigger jobs than I ever held. So, if you find yourself doubting whether a prospective hire is the right fit, make sure you're not hesitating because you fear he or she might draw the spotlight away from you. Hire the absolute best. Their brilliance will not diminish your reputation; it will make you shine even brighter.

8. Describe the job completely. Candidates should know exactly what they'll be signing up for if they join your organization. You owe it to them, and to your company, to provide every detail about the responsibility, authority, and accountability they'll have if hired and to give them a good sense of the company culture.

At the Disney hiring center, which is called Casting, a video is shown to all potential hires before they are interviewed. The movie highlights the Disney heritage and traditions; provides an overview of the compensation plan, benefit package, and perks; and describes the policy on scheduling and other practical issues. It also outlines what the company expects by way of professionalism, right down to the strict grooming standards that Cast Members are held to. Some applicants get up and leave without bothering with the interview. The film not only serves as a great orientation for eventual employees but also saves the company the high cost of hiring, training, and replacing people who would ultimately prove to be wrong for the job.

That idea has been adopted by a number of companies who learned about it through the Disney Institute. One of them is Mercedes Homes, a construction company based in Florida that has sent nearly three hundred employees to the institute for custom-designed programs. At one of those seminars Stuart McDonald, corporate VP of operations, asked, "How does Disney make sure that it hires the right people?" When he was told about the preinterview video, Stuart hired a film company to produce one for Mercedes Homes. "We find that about fifteen percent of the applicants watch it and hand back the application without filling it out," he says. "People who won't live up to the standards disqualify themselves, so we don't have to struggle with the mistakes they'd make or the bad impression they'd give." And guess what? The employee turnover rate plummeted and referral rates went up—as did morale, pride, and camaraderie.

Funny thing is, some companies discover benefits before they even produce the video. When Marylynne Kelts, the director of service excellence at Saint Agnes Medical Center in Fresno, California, decided to produce a preapplication video, she quickly realized that the company would have to do some serious thinking about its standards before it could clearly state in the video what it expected of employees. That process led to a guidebook that's given to all employees, as well as a systematic program in which one specific standard is featured company-wide for an entire month. As of the time I write this, the company has not yet produced the video, but defining the standards that will be outlined in it has already produced dividends in performance and productivity.

What are *your* standards? Exactly what is expected of your employees? Make sure every applicant gets the full picture before either of you makes a decision you might come to regret.

9. Check out candidates personally. In 1979, two years into my tenure as director of food and beverage at the Chicago Marriott, I was called to company headquarters in Washington, D.C., to meet with the regional vice president, Al Lefaivre. I was being considered for a promotion, and I was ready to let him know about all the things I'd accomplished in Chicago. But before I could even open my mouth, he told me that he already knew—and not just by reputation. Al had actually checked into the hotel for three days to check out the restaurants, banquets, bars, and room service under my supervision. "Your operation is a reflection of you," he told me. I got the job—and the message.

Ever since then, whenever possible, I have personally checked out candidates for important positions, and I've encouraged other leaders to do the same. Anyone can look great on paper and have references that sing his or her praises to the sky, but people are only as good as the results they achieve, so you owe yourself and your company a good close look. If possible, visit his or her current place of business and observe the operations carefully. Are the employees competent and well trained? Do they look and act professional? Are they efficient and organized? Are the facilities clean? Listen in on conversations, and try to talk directly to the people who worked with the candidate. What you see and hear reflects what the person will bring to your organization.

Some of the most important hiring decisions I've made were the result of such field trips. For example, when Disney World was planning to open the BoardWalk Inn Resort (a hotel fashioned after the early Boardwalk in Atlantic City), we decided it made financial sense to contract certain food and drink operations to outside parties, but only if they met our standards. One restaurant company gave us a very persuasive audiovisual presentation showing its excellence at running the type of operation we were planning. But we didn't take it at its word. One Wednesday night my colleague Bud Dare and I drove to Jacksonville, a five-hour round-trip journey, to see what kind of place the company was running. We hadn't even parked the car when the first red flag went up: A parking lot attendant asked for a payoff to let us park closer to the restaurant entrance. Then we noticed that the glass door was dirty, and there were cigarette butts on the floor. We had to wait a long time to be greeted, and when we finally ate, the service and the food were mediocre. The grimy bathroom was the last straw. Clearly, the management of that company did not have the same standards as Disney. Needless to say, it didn't get the contract.

That's an example of when a field trip averted disaster. On most occasions the visits led to the opposite outcome; I hired key personnel after seeing how *well* they ran their current operations. No matter the result, every plane ticket, hotel bill, and hour out of my schedule was a worthwhile investment.

Obviously, when candidates are unemployed, you can't witness their work firsthand. But you still have to dig below the surface, all the way to the real reasons they left their last employers. Good leaders usually stay in an organization or leave on their own. If your candidate was laid off, find out why. Don't accept euphemisms like "He left to pursue other opportunities." This is like political appointees leaving office to "spend more time with the family." The message is: "We don't want you to know the real reason he or she was asked to leave."

That a candidate is currently unemployed should not be a disqualifier. I've hired a number of people who had been let go from their previous jobs, and they worked out great. But you are well advised to probe for the real reasons the person was dismissed before making your decision.

10. Ask revealing questions. When you're interviewing potential hires, don't just ask predictable questions with yes or no answers. Toss in surprises that require thoughtful explanations. Some of my favorite questions have been:

* How do you stay on top of the labor costs in your organization?

* What's the best idea you ever came up with to improve your business?

* How do you plan your day?

Posing hypothetical situations is a great way to see if people can think on their feet. I've asked, for instance, "What would you do if you found out your boss was doing something illegal or unethical?" and "What would you do if your boss told you not to hire a candidate because of his or her race?" You can learn an awful lot from someone's response to questions like those, especially if you probe deeper than the initial answer, which might reflect what he or she thinks you want to hear. Don't let anyone off the hook that easily.

I will never forget the answer I got from a candidate I interviewed for an executive position. As I mentioned earlier, I highly value self-organization, and I plan each day in great detail, assigning priorities to my work to make sure I get the right things done in the right order. So I asked this candidate to explain how he planned his day. To my surprise he said, "I just wait for something to happen, and then I try to fix it." I knew then and there that he and I would be a really bad match. I hired someone who knew that good planning helps you prevent fires so you don't spend all your time putting them out.

11. Use structured interviews when possible. As I mentioned in number 6 above, structured interviews are a great way to uncover what you really need to know about people: how they think and how they lead. Conducted by trained psychologists over the phone, the interviews probe into areas that ordinary interviews can't reach and create detailed profiles— sometimes as long as ten pages—assessing the candidates' strengths and "areas of opportunity" in categories such as teamwork, courage, and critical thinking. By sorting out how people think and feel and by identifying the subtle talents they have and those they lack, these profiles give you a much clearer idea of what you'll really get if you hire one of them.

At Disney we discovered this powerful tool in 1994. Having made some costly hiring errors, we needed to find a better way to screen potential leaders. After researching the area thoroughly, we contracted with Jan Miller of the Gallup Organization to conduct structured interviews for every managerial position. We liked the results so much that we had Gallup create profiles of our current executives as well. I don't mind telling you, reading my own profile taught me an awful lot about myself, and it helped me become a better leader. Whether you have them done by Gallup or another company, you will find that profiles expertly conducted are a valuable investment.

12. Find out what really matters to your applicants. At Disney we needed to know if potential Cast Members could work on weekends or holidays, our busiest times. But I was suspicious of candidates who were *too* willing to sacrifice their families and private lives for the sake of the company. I found that in the long run, balanced people with lives outside work were usually the best employees.

So take the time to find out what matters most to candidates; ask about their families and friends, as well as their hobbies, passions, and leisure interests. People are often reluctant to bring up their personal lives because they think it's irrelevant or inappropriate or because they want to portray a total commitment to their jobs. One way to open them up is to talk about yourself. You'd be surprised how glad they'll be to find out you have a life and that you care about theirs. It sure worked for me. When I met with Al Weiss about the position that brought me to Orlando, I quickly learned that he shared my strong belief in work-life balance. Knowing that my boss would be agreeable to my going to the gym every afternoon and attending all my family events helped persuade Priscilla and me to give up Paris.

Throughout my years at Walt Disney World, I followed Al's example. For instance, when a young mother named Jeanette Manent came to work as a secretary, I told her that I expected her to go to all school events, no matter what the day or time. I added that if there was an event that very week, she should not be too intimidated to ask for time off, even though she was just starting her new job in my office. A few months later Jeanette asked for two months off to be with her father, who was dying of cancer. I said that her position would be waiting for her when she returned, and it was. Over the years we found that her loyalty and commitment to her family were mirrored in her loyalty and commitment to Disney. She continues to be a prized Cast Member to this day and was recently promoted to an administrative assistant position.

Remember, well-rounded people who want balanced lives will ultimately be more productive than workaholics with no interests outside the office.

13. If possible, have candidates demonstrate their expertise. I once interviewed an applicant for a pastry chef's job who said she was an expert in wedding cakes. That was very appealing, but candidates' opinions of their own gifts are no more reliable than their résumés. So I sent her to the pastry shop and told her to make a three-tier wedding cake. She was even better than she said she was. Watching her work with icing was like watching Michelangelo sculpt marble, and the result was as delicious as it was beautiful. We hired her on the spot. If we hadn't seen and tasted her work ourselves, someone else might have snapped her up instead.

On another occasion, I gave a potential chef four hours to round up the ingredients and cook the best hamburger and fries he could. I will never, ever forget the juiciness of the meat, the perfectly toasted bun, the center-cut tomatoes, and the fabulous slice of red onion cut to just the right size and thickness, not to mention the deliciously seasoned mayonnaise and Dijon mustard. Needless to say, he was hired, and I ate in his restaurant every chance I could get.

Obviously, you can't ask all professionals to demonstrate their skills. That's where other strategies mentioned here—onsite visits, creative interviewing, structured profiles, etc.—come into play. But whenever possible, give candidates an opportunity to strut their stuff.

14. Select the best candidate, not the best one available.
Experts have said that American companies are too quick to hire and too slow to fire. Far too often leaders act as though they were in the business of filling jobs quickly, rather than of filling them with the very best people and then developing them for greater responsibility. So don't succumb to a false sense of urgency, thinking, "I have to pick one of these available people so I can fill this job right away," or, "This selection process is taking up too much time. Let's get it over with." Take all the time you need—for your sake, for the candidates' sake, for the sake of the people who have to work with them, and for the sake of your organization.

I can't tell you how many mistakes I made early in my career because I hired people too rashly. Back then most of the interviews I conducted lasted less than an hour. I believed everything the candidates told me and didn't bother to talk to their references or make sure their résumés were 100 percent accurate. Eventually I wised up and learned to do my homework and hold out until I found the very best person.

Be warned, taking your time about hiring is not always popular with colleagues. In the mid-nineties, we needed to hire a new VP to run Downtown Disney. There was an awful lot of pressure to hurry up and fill that important slot, but I wouldn't be rushed. Over the course of six months, we flew a dozen candidates to Orlando for extensive interviews and conducted thorough background and reference checks on each one. Most of them had terrific credentials and had worked in the right places, but no one was quite right: Either the person's Gallup profile pointed to a leadership style that gave me pause, or he or she lacked an important skill set. One person wasn't organized, another was weak in measurement skills, a few lacked relationship strengths, and so on. About five months into this process the VP to whom the new person was to report ran out of patience. She wanted to hire *someone* and was willing to settle for the best available candidate. But I held out. I *knew* there was a better leader out there, and sure enough, one day Karl Holz came along. Karl possessed strong technical knowledge of the theme park business, plus outstanding financial skills and an excellent background; he had been the CEO of an airline catering company. One of the best hires I ever made, Karl went on to become the president of Disney Cruise Line and the chairman and CEO of Disneyland Paris.

Remember, in the long run it's better to put in the extra work than to fill slots with the wrong people. After all, think about how much time you'll waste cleaning up the messes made by unqualified hires—not to mention having to go through the hiring process all over again if you have to let unsuitable people go.

What if you're on the fence about hiring someone and you're getting impatient? Try this: Imagine that the person is *your* leader. Can you see yourself working for him or her? If you can't, then keep on looking. I knew I had mastered the art of hiring once every person who reported to me was someone I would gladly report to myself.

15. Look for people to nurture and promote. Every point we've discussed about hiring the right people also applies to promotions. Great leaders always have their antennae out for people to elevate to leadership positions, and they use every tool available to guide their selections.

A few years into my tenure at Walt Disney World, I was struck by a bolt of common sense: Maybe we weren't seeing the trees for the forest. Among the tens of thousands of frontline Cast

Members, there had to be a great many individuals who had the potential to be managers, and we should identify them and prepare them for leadership. So we created a series of mandatory one-hour training sessions for all five thousand managers in operations. We brought them into a ballroom a thousand at a time and told them it was their responsibility to find potential managers hidden in our workforce. But how? First the managers would have one-on-one meetings with every person who worked for them and look for signs of leadership potential: intelligence, self-direction, initiative, good relationship skills, high energy, and positive attitude. We told them to find curious people who strove for performance excellence; who wanted to grow and learn and take on more responsibility; who went to school and took classes to better themselves; who were always reliable, on time, and didn't whine when they were asked to stay late or come in early. We also told them to find out which frontline Cast Members played the role of go-to person for their coworkers, since groups tend to self-select people with natural leadership skills.

Soon virtually every manager in the company had become an eagle-eyed talent scout. Their efforts helped us populate the leadership with skilled, motivated, and inspired leaders—mainly from within the company.

Many Cast Members didn't even know their own potentials until a manager or executive spotted them. Once, at a round-table meeting with frontline Cast Members, I noticed a bright and enthusiastic young woman by the name of Odette Farmer. A single mother without a college degree, Odette was primarily concerned with holding a steady job and providing for her daughter. She didn't see herself as a leader, but I saw it plain as day. After the meeting I found out that Erin Wallace had the same impression. Odette was special, whether she knew it or not. So with the help of her management team we made sure Odette was nurtured, encouraged, and trained. Before long she was promoted to a management position, and sure enough, she became a terrific leader. I still run into her from time to time, and she always says she can't believe how much she has achieved since Erin and I "discovered" her.

I'll tell you what I told my managers at Disney and what I tell audiences at my speeches today: If you think back to playing hide-and-seek as a child, you'll remember that when you hid, before long you started to make noise or move around. Why? Because you wanted to be found. So do the future managers hiding in your organizations. It's your job as a leader to find them.

16. *Constantly evaluate performance.* In your ongoing search for leaders within your organization, you can't get more reliable information than you get from your employees. Here's how that valuable feedback is gathered at Disney. Once a year everyone fills out a Cast excellence survey that asks exactly what he or she thinks and feels about work environments, colleagues, and immediate leaders. The survey consists of more than a hundred statements, each rated on a seven-point scale— from "strongly agree" to "strongly disagree," for example, or "never" to "always." Here are some sample items about the organizational culture.

 ✳ I trust the people in my work team.

 ✳ I receive the training I need to do my job well.

 ✳ My work team values different points of view.

 ✳ My immediate leader deals with me in a truthful manner.

* My immediate leader makes the best use of my talents and skills to accomplish team goals.

* My immediate leader accepts responsibility for failures as well as successes.

* I trust my leader.

* If given the choice, I would work with my immediate leader again.

In addition to yielding valuable information about who leads well and who might need extra training, surveys offer a key fringe benefit: They tell employees that you care about what they think. One year we decided not to survey everyone in operations. We thought we could save time by distributing the survey only to a few people from a cross section of departments. *Big mistake!* Cast Members told us in no uncertain terms that they did not appreciate our taking away their opportunity to give their opinions. I issued a public apology and never made that same mistake again.

17. Recognize when the job doesn't fit the talent. Ideally, you will become so skilled at selecting and promoting the right people that you'll be able to fill every position with someone who fits the culture to a T. But let's face it, no one is perfect, and neither is any system or procedure. Sometimes, despite your efforts, you'll find you've filled a round hole with a square peg.

Figuring out what to do with employees who don't fit is one of the hardest things for leaders to do, yet it's one of the most important things for them to do. Like an actor cast in the wrong part, if an employee is clearly unable to perform his or her role, you have to do what directors do: Replace the person with someone more appropriate, or else the whole performance will bomb. Needless to say, the best course of action is to transfer the employee to a position in the company where he or she *can* perform well. If you handle it right, moving someone to a more suitable position will prove best for that employee as well as the organization. After all, if someone is stuck in a job that calls upon talents he or she doesn't have, it usually means he or she is *not* using the talents he or she *does* have.

At Disney we thought that if people were good enough to be hired or promoted in the first place, they deserved to be given another chance to excel. At one point we promoted a highly competent director to a newly created position with the title of vice president. It appeared that having run a business operation at his previous company, he had the necessary experience. But we didn't realize that the new job required more technical expertise than he had. For two miserable years he tried to solve problems he wasn't equipped to deal with. Finally, my colleagues and I realized what he already knew: He simply was not cut out for the role. So with his cooperation, we moved him into an operating role, similar to the one he'd had before the promotion, where he could use his natural talent for managing people. He was happier and more productive, and he is doing an extraordinary job to this day.

The signs of a bad fit include not being able to complete one's work, being consistently late with assignments, poor reviews from one's direct reports, low ratings on customer satisfaction scales, complaints about one's attitude from coworkers, frequent absences, and a decline in measurable business results. If you see such signs, deal with the situation right away; don't wait for the employee to recognize the problem and request a transfer. People who are promoted to an ill-fitting position usually know pretty quickly that it's not their thing, but they don't necessarily speak up. For one thing, they might be too embarrassed to admit it; for another, they like the salary, prestige, and perks of the new position.

There are of course times when a person's performance can be improved through training and mentoring. But that's not what I'm talking about here. I'm talking here about people who, no matter how hard they try or how much support they receive, are just not right for the roles in which they've been cast. It's up to you as a leader to take the appropriate action: Offer assistance to those who need more time or help, and for those who don't fit the jobs they were placed in, work hard to find them positions where they can add value. If you've created an inclusive environment in which problems can be discussed honestly, you should be able to correct the situation before it deteriorates and termination is your only option. In any sizable organization where people are respected and valued, it's usually not too difficult to find a more suitable role for a talented person.

18. Terminate quickly and kindly. Naturally, there are times when you can't find an appropriate place for someone who no longer has value in his or her current position. Letting him or her go is extremely tough, but in the long run it's usually best for everyone to do so.

To this day I remember how awful I felt the first time I had to fire a manager for poor performance. It was at the Chicago Marriott. I had actively recruited that man, and I'd talked him into leaving his old company to come work for me. But he just didn't work out. His department was disorganized, his labor costs were out of line, he could not control expenses, and he did not deal well with poor performers. As a result, many banquet functions did not start on time, causing enormous dissatisfaction among our guests. I postponed firing him, put it off some more, and then a little longer, until one day my own boss said that I'd be fired if I didn't take action. When I finally bit the bullet and met with the man, I beat around the bush for quite some time before I finally told him I had to let him go. I'm ashamed to say that I also blamed the decision on someone else.

All in all, it was a great example of how not to fire someone. Years later I heard this saying in a seminar: "A leader's job is to do what has to be done, when it has to be done, in the way it should be done, whether you like it or not and whether they like it or not." I found that precept incredibly inspiring, and I call upon it whenever I have to do something I'd rather not do. I also learned from early mistakes that once a decision is made to terminate someone, a strong leader acts quickly. Needless delays do not spare the person an ounce of pain, and they certainly don't do your stress level any good. In fact, it makes for a toxic workplace. If someone is not performing well, you owe it to everyone on the team, as well as the company as a whole, to change the lineup as quickly and efficiently as possible.

As I discuss in the previous chapter, it is essential that leaders manage termination with kindness and compassion. When you break the news to a good person who is no longer a good fit, do it face-to-face, and make the announcement as soon as you sit down. But your responsibility as a leader doesn't end there. Unless there has been malfeasance of some kind, you should take as long as necessary to explain exactly *why* the decision was made. Remember, decent people are owed a decent explanation and, if possible, a good lesson to take away from the bitter experience.

19. *Don't lose touch with those you lose.* As we've seen, sometimes you have to terminate employees who don't have the right skills or whose skills no longer fit. But the opposite can also occur: Sometimes you lose people because they become *too* skilled. They outgrow their positions and become frustrated because they can't fully utilize their talents. Regrettably, I lost such people several times during my career, and I'm sad to say it can't always be prevented. One terrific executive left because he had not been given the responsibility and authority to run a Disney business. He fully deserved that opportunity, but we had no way to give it to him at the time, so he moved to another company. It was a huge loss, but it taught me a valuable lesson: Do everything possible to reconfigure the organization's structure to suit its talent. Of course a structural fix can't always be made immediately, so I let those discontented people know that we understood their frustration and were committed to finding a solution. I tried to convince them to be patient until we could give them the opportunity they deserved, and I'd suggest reasonable increases in salary and responsibility to make things better for them in the interim.

Still, when people outgrow their positions, you can't always keep them around. Sometimes they get tired of waiting, and other times they get offered desirable positions elsewhere. That brings me to another lesson I learned at Disney: Keep in touch with great employees who leave. We did exactly that with the executive I just described. Because he stayed in the area, someone from our executive team occasionally had dinner or drinks with him and talked about life and work. Two years later we rehired him, for exactly the kind of position he wanted. He's still happily employed at Disney World, and I'm sure that before long he'll be promoted to an even higher level.

These days there are myriad ways to stay in touch with people and to keep relationships alive, so you have a shot at bringing them back to your organization one day. With e-mail, voice mail, cell phones, and the good old post office, you really have no excuse for not keeping track of high-potential people you might want to work with again.

The bottom line is this: No matter what kind of company you run, your people are your brand; if you don't have good people, no amount of marketing, advertising, or PR will make up for it. This is why it is crucial for you as a leader to learn how to hire, promote, and nurture the very best people out there. Trust me, it pays off in both employee satisfaction and measurable business results.

ACTION STEPS

✳ Make sure candidates have the technical, management, and leadership skills they need to do an excellent job.

✳ Think about what the perfect candidate would look like before you start recruiting new employees or promoting from within.

✳ Select by talent, not by résumé.

✳ Select the best person for the job, not the best one available.

✳ Consider carefully how a potential hire will blend in with the current team.

* Involve team members at all levels in the interview and selection process.

* Utilize structured interviews where appropriate.

* Ask candidates questions that require thoughtful answers instead of just yes or no.

* Speak at length and in depth with people who have worked for or with the candidate.

* Observe the work the candidate currently does or the operation the candidate currently manages.

* Quiz candidates on their knowledge, and if possible, have them demonstrate their expertise.

* Be willing to make difficult decisions about removing or reassigning talent that isn't the right fit.

CHAPTER SIX

STRATEGY #4

CREATE MAGIC
THROUGH TRAINING

After Hurricane Charley struck Orlando in 2004, I received a letter from a top executive of an insurance company that insured *Walt Disney World*® Resort. By coincidence, he had been staying at Disney's Yacht Club and Beach Club Resort as the storm approached. Now he was writing to tell me how impressed he was by how Cast Members had hustled to take precautionary measures like tying down every loose item on the property. The insurance executive said he originally thought he'd seen a lapse in Disney's preventive planning—no one had secured the chairs and table on his terrace—but when he returned to his room from dinner, those items were sitting inside his room, along with a note saying they'd be returned to the terrace when the hurricane passed. And to his surprise, one of the people doing the heavy lifting was Sam Pensula, the hotel's general manager, whom he spotted among the Cast Members placing sandbags in front of certain doors to keep water out of the hotel. He wrote that in all his years in the insurance business he had never seen such careful preparation for a natural disaster.

When an organization can perform that well in a crisis, it's because its employees have been thoroughly trained. Every single Cast Member at Walt Disney World had rehearsed the emergency preparedness plan many times, and all of them played their roles to perfection. That rigorous preparation not only saved lives and property but paid off financially. We opened for business the morning after the deluge, and we didn't even meet the deductible on the insurance policy.

Once you have the right people in place, your task as a leader is to give them everything they need to excel. My son, Daniel, once told me, "Dad, you can't fire your children; you have to develop them." Well, if leaders applied that wisdom to their employees, they'd find that a lot fewer of them quit or get fired. Like good parents, good leaders prepare their people to take on future responsibilities by providing appropriate educational opportunities and exposing them to important developmental experiences.

If you think that training and development are the exclusive role of human resources or some other department and that you are too busy to bother with them, you might want to rethink what it means to be a leader. Consider this story I'm fond of telling to managers. A father says to his daughter, "What do you want to be when you grow up?" She answers, "I want to be a teacher." The father says, "But, honey, don't you really want to be a doctor like me? Doctors are very important. Without doctors many people would get sick and suffer." "But daddy," says the little girl, "without teachers there would be no doctors!"

I assure you neither your personal success nor your paycheck will give you the same satisfaction as seeing the people you lead achieve their goals and aspirations. The leaders at Walt Disney World have found that to be true. Training and development permeate every level of the company; they are the primary reason the Disney brand is synonymous with service excellence. The learning journey for all new Cast Members begins with a course called Traditions, which educates them about the company's history and its legacy of superlative Guest service. Once Cast Members begin to feel the pixie dust of Disney magic and realize they're part of a unique corporate culture, they start learning how to perform their roles. Having learned such basic lessons as the importance of being friendly toward Guests, smiling, and keeping the environment clean, they proceed with careful on-the-job training. About sixty days later, once they're comfortable with their basic skills, they learn how to perform the technical aspects of their roles, which vary according to their specific tasks. Then they are taught how to exceed Guest expectations, using the principles in this chapter.

I'm often asked what Disney means by exceeding Guest expectations. I say it consists of small, thoughtful, individualized acts of magic, performed by employees for customers. Let me give you an example. As I was writing this chapter, I attended a conference for Travelers Insurance in Savannah, Georgia. The director of human resources told me how on a recent visit to Walt Disney World she'd learned what exceeding expectations meant. When she checked out of her hotel, the front desk host asked if she would like to keep the key card to her room as a souvenir for her child. She said she would like that, but that she had twins and couldn't possibly bring home a gift for one and not the other. So the desk clerk made a key card for each child, with their names printed on them. *That* is exceeding Guest expectations.

Disney's training programs are designed and executed by expert professionals, and they are often facilitated by specially trained Cast Members. Managerial training is longer and more extensive, culminating in both written and practical assessments. In food and beverage, for instance, everyone from dishwashers to chefs to managers receives rigorous training and is thoroughly tested in procedures before he or she even lifts a plate without supervision. If you eat at any Disney restaurant, you'll find that every server knows every ingredient in every dish on the menu. This has advantages beyond enabling him or her to answer ordinary questions from diners. If you say that your child has a certain food allergy, for example, the server will bring the chef to your table to consult with you about how he or she can prepare a safe meal. Because of that special training, many parents of allergic children come only to Disney resorts for vacations. And if you're a wine buff, that same server will be able to answer your every question about the wine list; about a quarter of the twenty-five hundred certified sommeliers in America work at Walt Disney World, which sells more wine than any single site in the world.

In addition to formal training, *informal learning* is emphasized every minute of every day. Disney leaders are given extensive resources to help Cast Members learn and grow continuously. As in Hollywood, the company knows that the next superstar can come from anywhere, so the culture encourages the nurturing of future leaders. Cast Members with leadership potential receive a thorough grounding in what is expected of a Disney manager, followed by active on-the-job mentoring and access to a wide range of educational resources in the company's Learning Centers. Staffed by the equivalent of reference librarians, these small, conveniently located resource libraries are open to any Cast Member who wishes to take advantage of development opportunities, from online language courses to technical training. Self-paced training programs geared to helping Cast Members become more effective in their work can be accessed on the company Intranet. Some, like the courses in ethics and various legal issues, are mandatory. Others are strictly voluntary, but everyone who aspires to advance in his or her career is strongly encouraged to take advantage of them. In many cases, managers work directly with the learning and development department to design individual learning plans for potential leaders.

Disney training also takes full advantage of other cutting-edge technology. For example, computer simulation is used to teach drivers to maneuver vehicles through an Animal Kingdom attraction while reciting a script and answering questions. And when housekeepers are taught how to make beds using a device that cuts down on back injuries, they use iPods to watch the process on-screen and listen to instructions through earphones, while trying it themselves at the same time.

As someone who owes his career to leaders who took the time to help him grow, I know that educating employees pays off big-time. If you make sure people know how to do their jobs well and show that you care about their future, you'll not only improve their performances but also bolster their self-confidence and inspire in them a profound sense of commitment. So give your people everything they need to excel by developing effective, thorough, consistent training processes and learning opportunities. Here are some tips that will help you accomplish that, beginning with the most important principle of all.

1. Give people a purpose, not just jobs. Back when Orlando was still a sleepy town, Walt Disney wrote the following to the leadership of his young theme park in Anaheim, California:

"Here at Disneyland we meet our world public on a person-to-person basis for the first time. Your every action (and mine as well) is a direct reflection of our entire organization." That spirit of purpose has been instilled ever since in each individual who works at what became the biggest resort business in the world.

In most workplaces, people know what their jobs are and are prepared to do what's expected of them. Most managers are content with that. But for great leaders and great companies, that's not enough. Their people don't just show up in the morning and do what is asked of them; they *want* to be there, they're proud to be there, and they reach above and beyond, constantly raising the bar of excellence. Why? Because their leaders don't just give them jobs; they inspire them with a higher sense of purpose.

I learned the importance of giving people a purpose when I managed the Marriott in Springfield, Massachusetts. Our business was coasting along quite well when suddenly a more luxurious hotel was built across the street. Forced to respond to this competitive challenge without undergoing a long and costly overhaul, I decided to focus on service. My philosophy—one that applies to *any* business—was that all customers deserved the best possible service, even though they might pay different rates for different amenities. If you give them quality service, they're far more likely to leave satisfied and to return again and again. In fact, studies show that the primary reason businesses lose customers is not inadequate products and services but the way they treat people.

To inspire my staff to reach for a higher level of service, I created a purpose statement that was so simple no one would ever forget it: "Be so nice to our guests that they won't believe it."

That statement was taken to heart by everyone from house-keepers to managers. I knew it was working when a guest came into my office one morning and said he was so blown away by the service he'd received that he was bringing an entire convention group to the hotel. It seems that when he checked in late the previous night, he'd asked if he could get a banana to eat before bed. The desk clerk said she was sorry but the kitchen was closed. Disappointed, the guest went to the bar for a drink. Then the desk clerk saw that purpose statement hanging on the wall. She went straight to the kitchen, found two bananas, and placed them in the guest's room with a note.

At Walt Disney World, I heard dozens of stories like that every week from Guests who wanted to express appreciation, and often amazement, because a Cast Member did something extraordinary for them. The funny thing is, people spend thousands of precious dollars on food, lodging, transportation, and entertainment, but what they mostly remember, and write letters about, are things like the bus driver who made them laugh and the housekeeper who left little surprises in the room for their children.

Disney leaders are trained to make sure that every single Cast Member understands the difference between his or her specific role and the purpose that's shared by everyone in the company. I boiled that purpose down to this statement: "Make sure that every Guest has the most fabulous time of his or her life."

That sentence tells Cast Members exactly what the ultimate outcome of their work must be. Their jobs may be vastly different, but everyone from custodians to vice presidents is guided by the spirit of that purpose statement. You can see it in the behavior of "onstage" Cast Members, those who interact directly with Guests, and in the attitude of the "backstage" Cast, those who keep the operation running behind the scenes. You can see it as well in the decisions made by managers and executives every day.

The company also uses three longer statements that add powerful substance to that concise expression of purpose:

The Vision Statement: What We Want to Be. Walt Disney World will always be dedicated to making dreams come true. In this magical world, fantasy is real and reality is fantastic. A wonderful sense of community awaits where all are greeted as welcome Guests who become cherished friends. For all who work and play here, Walt Disney World will be a source of joy and inspiration.

The Essence Statement: What We Want Our Guests to Feel. Walt Disney World is a magical passage into a world of fantasy and adventure. Here we can wish upon a star, experience the impossible and bring our dreams to life. Together, treasured friends discover a wonderland that dazzles, delights, and renews through all the seasons of a lifetime.

The Mission Statement: What We Must Do. Our mission is to honor our heritage and continually reinvent Walt Disney World . . .

* By making dreams come true, creating magical memories and developing lifetime friendships with each Guest.

* By valuing, respecting and trusting each other as dream makers and honoring our individuality, ability and contributions as Cast Members.

* By fostering a fun and enriching environment in which creativity, teamwork, openness, diversity, courage, balance and accountability are celebrated.

* By being innovative and embracing new ideas.

* By eliminating bureaucracy and all the barriers that get in the way of operating simply, quickly and efficiently.

* By achieving the financial successes that will enable us to grow and fulfill our Vision.

I'm sure that very few Cast Members remember all that. No doubt, many of them can't recite even the one-line purpose statement verbatim. But thanks to constant reinforcement from leaders who walk their talk, they all internalize the meaning of every word. For example, when a couple once told a restaurant server that they'd lost their child's pacifier and the hotel store was closed, the server tracked down the manager, got the keys to the store, and brought a brand-new pacifier to their room. Another time a merchandise Cast Member overheard a Guest tell his wife that he'd left his cell phone charger at home; she went to Wal-Mart the next day—her day off—and bought one for him. And when, on a rainy day in the Magic Kingdom, a Cast Member saw that a little girl had wet her pants and the family didn't have time to go to their room to change her clothes, he took them to a store, got them a voucher for a free replacement outfit, and provided them with a place to change her clothes. None of these Cast Members was required to do these things. They *wanted* to do them because they understood their purpose.

These are a tiny fraction of the true stories I heard during my years at Disney. I assure you they are par for the course. They can and should be in your business as well, no matter what your product or service may be. For example, at Mercedes Homes, the construction firm I introduced in the previous chapter, the leaders who attended Disney Institute programs began to train employees in their purpose, not just their jobs. Among the many payoffs was this heartwarming story. A frontline service manager who was doing community service work came across a woman with five children whose house had burned down. Because Mercedes had built her house, the employee felt moved to do something about the family's plight. He went to the company executives, who contacted the producers of the TV show *Extreme Makeover: Home Edition*. The show paid for Mercedes to build the family a new seven-thousand-square-foot house.

So dig deep and ask yourself exactly what your purpose is. When you've captured it in a succinct and inspiring statement, trumpet it repeatedly, and reflect it in your own behavior as well. Don't be satisfied with printing a mission statement in your brochures and annual reports or hanging it on the wall in the reception area. Make sure all your employees absorb it in their hearts and minds. When they know deep down what they're aiming for each day, their every decision and action will be infused with that purpose.

2. Take your role as a teacher seriously. If you want to be surrounded by great employees, being a teacher, coach, and counselor is far more effective than just being a boss. Earn a reputation as a good teacher, and people will line up to work for you. If you help other leaders become good teachers as well, you'll multiply your value.

Remember, *who* does the teaching is just as important as *what* is being taught. For instance, lots of people can teach a seminar out of a manual, but people with expertise and experience in the topic bring something extra. When I taught my monthly time management course at Disney World, it carried extra credibility because everyone knew I practiced time management exactly the way I taught it. The course was wildly popular with everyone from frontline staff to top executives, and because of its success, Disney soon started a program called Executives as Coaches, in which leaders offered classes in their areas of expertise. So, for example, two vice presidents in finance, Jim Lewis and Stephanie Janik, taught a six-hour finance course that was consistently full. I myself took it and learned a tremendous amount. Greg Emmer, who has been with Disney for more than thirty-five years, taught a well-attended course on company heritage and culture, and Dieter Hannig taught nutrition and exercise. Dieter was not only our food and beverage expert, but as someone who ran twenty miles for fun on Saturdays he was known as the healthiest executive at Disney. Because these executives were teaching subjects they considered important, they took their roles as teachers that much more seriously, and the result was well-informed Cast Members who were grateful for the opportunities to learn.

3. Become a COACH. I've found the acronym COACH—care, observe, act, communicate, help—to be a great guide for training and developing employees:

Care. Show your team members you care by focusing on everyone's individual development. Talk to them every day about excellence, and let them know what you are committed to and passionate about.

Observe. Close observation of the workplace will tell you what needs to be improved. Take some time every day to focus on your employees' behavior and work practices, and find out what each person needs to perform his or her role effectively.

Act. Timing is vital when you need to improve performance or behavior, and the best time is *now*. Model great leadership by taking action the minute you notice something that needs correcting.

Communicate. The best teachers are great communicators who find just the right way to get the attention of others. (There's more on communication later in the chapter.)

Help. Use your leadership position to help others become better. Show them how to perform tasks properly; be crystal clear about your expectations for performance, attitude, and behavior; and enforce the rules, policies, and operating guidelines.

Obviously, you can't spend all your time coaching. That's why training others to be teachers is vital. When we opened the World of Disney store, for instance, we added a position called Cast service manager, the sole purpose of which was to make sure frontline Cast Members were getting the support and training they needed. It was extremely effective, and the position is now being added to other operations across Walt Disney World.

4. Teach by example. Leaders who demand excellence need to model excellence, or else they have no credibility. I discovered early on that employees learned more from seeing me pick up a candy wrapper and carry it to a trash receptacle than from any lecture I could have given on maintaining a clean work environment. Also, I never asked people to do things I wasn't willing to do myself. I got coffee for employees rather than ask them to get it for me, and when a restaurant was short-handed, I rolled up my sleeves and helped out in the kitchen. They say a picture is worth a thousand words. Well, if you ask me, an action is worth even more. Your people will learn more from observing you than from what you tell them, so always lead by example. I read two quotes about parenting recently that also apply to business leaders: "You should not worry that your children are not listening to you. You should worry that they are always watching you" and "What you teach your children you teach *their* children."

In 1988, about a week into my tenure as general manager of the Springfield Marriott, I walked into the ballroom where we were about to serve a luncheon for three hundred guests and noticed a hole in one of the tablecloths caused by a cigarette burn (in those days people smoked in dining rooms). I called over the banquet captain and told her to change the tablecloth. She couldn't believe I asked her to do that. "I'll just cover the hole with a salt shaker," she said. I explained that seemingly minor details can make or break a company's—or a person's—entire reputation, and that was why we needed to pay attention to every little thing.

Ten years later, when I was at Walt Disney World, I received a letter from that banquet captain. She was now an important executive at a different company. Telling her to change that tablecloth was a turning point in her life, she told me. At the time, she thought I was unreasonable, if not totally crazy. But she watched me do "crazy" things like that for another two years, and one day she realized that I was engaged in an important act of leadership: teaching integrity and impeccable performance by modeling those values in everything I did. The purpose of her letter was to thank me for putting her on the path of learning how to lead.

5. Teach the principles of great service. No matter what kind of business or industry you're in, great service is critical to your company's success. At Walt Disney World, frontline Cast Members are taught the "7 Guest Service Guidelines," which establish a standard of friendly, courteous, considerate treatment for all Guests. To make the guidelines more memorable, each of the seven is associated with one of the Seven Dwarfs (see p. 129).

Like the company's statement of purpose, these service guidelines aren't just tacked up on a wall someplace; they are an integral part of the training that every Cast Member receives. Here's how.

* *Make eye contact and smile.* Cast Members are taught to begin and end every interaction with a Guest with direct eye contact and a sincere smile.

* *Greet and welcome each and every Guest.* Cast Members are trained to extend an appropriate greeting to every Guest they come into contact with, and specially themed greetings are even offered in different areas.

* *Seek out Guest contact.* Cast Members are expected to reach out to Guests who need assistance and to know all the necessary information, from first aid and safety procedures to the location of shops and restrooms.

* *Provide immediate service recovery.* Cast Members are trained in how best to resolve service problems, from

poorly prepared food to rooms that were not cleaned properly before check-in, and are taught how to rapidly find the appropriate information or person when they don't have the solution.

* *Display appropriate body language at all times.* Cast Members are coached in posture, facial expression, and other aspects of professional appearance to create the best impression on Guests.

* *Preserve the "magical" Guest experience.* All the training and development is geared toward teaching the Cast how to make Disney magic. Preserving that feeling of enchantment for the Guests has been a core value ever since the parks were first imagined by Walt Disney.

* *Thank each and every Guest.* Cast Members are taught to show appreciation to each and every Guest and to complete each and every interaction with a thank-you and a smile.

You don't have to be in the entertainment or hospitality business to provide a magical experience for the people your organization serves. You too can train employees in your organization in basic principles like these, and hi ho, hi ho, it's off to work they'll go, providing excellent service to your customers. Naturally, you don't have to use the same seven guidelines; create a set of standards that suits your circumstances by asking yourself what behaviors would make your customers go away happy. Leaders from a wide variety of organizations from all over the world have successfully adapted these very guidelines to their unique needs. For instance, after learning about the onstage/backstage concept at a Disney Institute program,

7 Guest
Service Guidelines

 Be *Happy*...make eye contact and smile!

 Be like *Sneezy*...greet and welcome each and every guest. Spread the spirit of Hospitality...It's contagious!

 Don't be *Bashful*...seek out Guest contact!

 Be like *Doc*...provide immediate Service recovery!

 Don't be *Grumpy*...always display appropriate body language at all times!

 Be like *Sleepy*...create DREAMS and preserve the "MAGICAL" Guest experience!

 Don't be *Dopey*...thank each and every Guest!

the owner of a supermarket chain made a rule that uniformed employees taking a break can hang out only "backstage." That way customers wouldn't see them smoking, snacking, and talking on their cell phones.

A number of companies have not only taught employees to apply Disney's service principles with customers but also adapted the standards to their internal training programs. For instance, Gold Fields Limited, a worldwide mining company based in South Africa, created the Mining School of Excellence in 2006 to upgrade and modernize the training of miners. Working with Disney Institute consultants, the school developed world-class programs ranging from basic technical skills to advanced leadership, and the primary shift was adopting what they call a service mind-set. "We realized that learners are customers," a Gold Fields executive said, "and we provided learning facilities that show them they are important and worthy of a well-equipped and clean venue." The company's new emphasis on treating "learners" with respect and courtesy included such specific changes as hiring a well-trained executive chef to provide healthy, high-quality food and attending to inquiries immediately instead of keeping learners waiting to be assisted for long periods of time outside offices. And as at Disney World, team members no longer walk past trash without cleaning it up.

For Gold Fields, the benefits of these changes reverberated well beyond having happier and better-trained employees. "The program facilitated a new way of doing our business," an executive said. "The standard we set at the Mining School impacted on the service standards of the rest of our company, and we witnessed the improvement of services and good manners being displayed at mining operations."

But remember, the best part is that these guidelines are only the beginning. Once your employees are trained in baseline service standards, they can be inspired to rise above them. At Disney, Cast Members are trained to fulfill not only conscious expectations but also the expectations that most Guests don't even realize they have. That's how good service becomes great service and great service becomes the kind of magical experience people never forget.

6. Train people for Magical Moments and Take 5s. At Walt Disney World, Magical Moments are planned events designed to engage the Guests and enhance their experience. For example, every morning a family waiting on line is chosen to open the park officially, and one of their children even gets to make the announcement. At certain attractions, Cast Members select a child to introduce a show, and every time a train departs in the Animal Kingdom, two kids are named assistant conductors and get to shout, "All aboard!" And during parades, Cast Members round up children to dance in the street with Mickey and Donald and other characters. It's not just the kids and their parents who love these moments; everyone watching loves them, and they rave about the experience when they go home.

Take 5s are more spontaneous. The Cast has been trained to seize opportunities to do something special for Guests: replace a spilled ice cream for free; walk an older person to the restroom; ask a little girl dressed like Cinderella for her autograph; tell a family something interesting about the park, like why there are special window displays on Main Street. Sometimes these moments are especially heartwarming, like the time a woman asked Mickey Mouse for an autograph to bring home to a little boy who was seriously ill. Mickey didn't just sign his name; he wrote a long personal letter in the child's autograph book.

Why are these individualized interactions called Take 5s?

Because they blow the Guests' minds in less than five minutes. Think of them as real-life versions of those random acts of kindness you read about on bumper stickers. At Disney they only *seem* random; the Cast Members are not only trained to look for Take 5 opportunities, but held accountable for making them happen.

Most Take 5s take closer to five seconds than five minutes, and from a business standpoint I can't imagine a better use of time. All those seconds and minutes repeated thousands of times a day add up to better customer relations than you could buy with a big corporate PR budget. A letter I once received from a mother expressed it best. "I was looking for magic in all the wrong places," she said. "Your staff is your magic."

You might be thinking, "It's easy for people at Disney World to do Take 5s and Magical Moments, but that kind of thing would never work in *my* business." Really? Think about the variety of human interactions that take place within your organization and between your employees and the outside world. Aren't there opportunities to make people feel a little more special? By teaching, coaching, and encouraging your employees to look for and seize these opportunities, you too can create extraordinary magic in your business.

7. Teach them how and where to spend their time. As a leader you need to make sure your employees know where to be and what to do under all circumstances—when it's busy and when it's slow, on an ordinary day and during a crisis. As a hotel executive, for instance, I made sure everyone knew to be at his or her assigned station, ready to greet Guests, when the ballroom doors opened for a function. When a restaurant opened for business, I made sure restaurant managers were in the dining room, not in their offices, and chefs were in the kitchen, not down in the storeroom or wine cellar. At Walt Disney World, attraction managers are trained to be at their attractions at key times to make certain all safety and operational guidelines are being followed, and merchandise managers are told to spend most of their time in the shops. Cast Members are trained not to hang out backstage or stand around talking to one another when things are slow; those downtimes are opportunities to organize or clean their areas or give more Guests individualized attention.

8. Communicate constantly. Use every means available to teach new lessons, share promising ideas and effective practices, reinforce important principles, announce research and survey data, and keep everyone up-to-date on organizational developments. Walt Disney World makes excellent use of a variety of communication vehicles that any company can emulate. Here are some examples.

A weekly newspaper. I started Disney's weekly paper, *The Main Street Diary*, in 2000, and I considered it so important that I took the time to write for every issue in my six remaining years with the company. To this day, come Friday at 5:00 P.M., Cast Members receive print or electronic versions of the paper. Every issue contained these features.

* Lee's Main Message to Leaders: a weekly message from the head of operations on how to be a better leader.

* Pre-Shift Meeting Message: suggestions on topics to cover in the daily pre-shift meeting (more on this in a minute).

* Do You Know: company news that Cast Members need to know about, like new hires, policies, promotions, etc.

* The Disney Difference: updates on perks and benefits for Cast Members.

* Advice from Mother: folksy tips on professional behavior.

* Safety Message of the Week: tips on how to maintain a safe environment.

* Security Message of the Week: how to stay alert for danger, along with phone numbers to contact in the event of an emergency.

* Your Community: local events and service opportunities.

* Respect for Diversity: lessons on creating an inclusive workplace.

* Main Reminders: messages regarding key policies and other matters.

* Important Dates: classes and events Cast Members might want to sign up for.

The feature I considered most valuable was the inspiring letters from actual Guests about Cast Members whose behavior had exceeded their expectations. People love this section of the newsletter and look forward each week to seeing whose names will be mentioned. Perhaps no other aspect of life at Walt Disney World did more for morale and team building during my time there than *The Main Street Diary*.

Pre-shift meetings. No matter what kind of company you run, one of the most effective ways to move employees along the learning curve is to hold brief, well-organized meetings before the start of operations each day. Just gather everyone around, and teach something new. Think about it: Ten minutes a day add up to more than forty hours of free education a year! Imagine what that much training would cost if you sent employees to a seminar for that long.

I gave every manager at Walt Disney World the following guidelines to help them think through their pre-shift meeting agendas. The heading was "Why Do We Have Pre-Shift Meetings?"

* To have two-way communication daily.

* To tell Cast Members what is important.

* To thank them for their great performance.

* To answer any questions.

* To provide product and service knowledge.

* To find out what they need to perform properly.

* To inspire them.

I also encouraged leaders to conduct skill and knowledge checks during pre-shift meetings. For example, they might say, "George, show the team how to present a bottle of wine and pour it properly," or, "Margot, what time does the Magic Kingdom close tonight, and what time are the fireworks?" or, "Tristan, what do you do if a Guest wants to cash a second-party check?" The purpose is to keep the team on its toes and help ensure that it learns what it needs to know.

Bulletin boards (the old-fashioned kind). It might sound antiquated in this electronic age, but if they're placed in the right location and kept fresh with interesting material, bulletin boards can be excellent communication tools. At Disney World they inform the Cast about everything from Guest satisfaction scores to details about the holiday party. Hung in a prominent place like a break area or cafeteria so Cast Members can't miss it, each board is assigned to one person who takes pride in making sure it's current and appealing to the eye.

One-on-ones. It is Disney World policy for every manager to schedule routine one-on-one discussions with each direct report. Some new managers balk at the requirement at first, but they soon discover that it's an invaluable way to communicate on a wide range of issues, from training needs to scheduling to process problems that need to be resolved. Perhaps most important, it is a way for leaders to demonstrate a genuine interest in each person and his or her aspirations.

9. Give feedback immediately and effectively. Feedback is a powerful method for training your employees, and that means first training yourself to always notice employee performance. Then quickly offer your feedback. Remember when you were a kid and you did something wrong? Your mother didn't wait for an annual review to let you know about it, did she? And when you did something really outstanding, like ace an exam or help your brother or sister with homework, your father didn't wait for a special occasion to give praise, did he? Well, even grown-ups learn best when the gap between action and feedback is short. What's more, most people are used to hearing from authority figures only when they do something wrong, so if you hold your constructive feedback for a regularly scheduled performance review to offer constructive criticism, your silence will be interpreted as approval. Just remember to be thoughtful and tactful, and never criticize someone in front of others.

I also suggest letting employees know what the organization as a whole is doing well and where it can stand improvement. At Disney, I issued periodic statements like these: "We have a problem keeping the areas around the queue lines clean when it is really busy, and I want you to focus on that" and "We're having difficulty getting people seated in the restaurants on time on Saturday nights, and we are working to improve that."

Your feedback will hit home more powerfully if you use effective instruction. For example, one very important teaching device is storytelling. Nothing better imparts more memorable lessons or inspires people to change their ways or spring into action than a tale well told. In fact, one reason Disney Institute programs are so effective is that its facilitators make use of Disney's tradition of great storytelling.

In my speeches and my one-on-one conversations I always draw on my life—past and present, at home and at work—to make important points. I've found stories about overcoming adversity or recovering from mistakes especially useful; too many leaders are afraid to admit mistakes, thinking it will undermine their credibility or be taken as weakness. But it's actually a great teaching tool. I think it's so important for leaders to let people know who they are, shortcomings and all, that I wrote a sixty-plus-page description of my career, including all the mistakes I'd made and the lessons I was forced to learn, then distributed that document to the entire Walt Disney World organization. It didn't bother me that people would know I'd been fired in the past and once had a reputation as a take-no-prisoners manager. Think of what they learned by knowing how I'd overcome those obstacles.

Here's another tip for giving feedback that people remember: Don't just tell it; explain it. As a parent I learned not just to command my son but to teach him the consequences of each course of action. When he was sixteen, Daniel got home one night at twelve-thirty, an hour later than he was supposed to. I told him I was upset, and like a typical teenager, he told me I was unfair. He accused me of wanting him home by eleven-thirty because I was sleepy. I explained that I had read about a study showing that car accidents go up by 35 percent after midnight, when most people leave bars. Daniel still did not like my rule, but once he knew the reason for it, he came to remember it and respect it. By contrast, when I was a kid my father would say, "You'll be home when I tell you," and if I asked why, he'd say, "Because I said so." I did not learn much from that.

Likewise, in business, whenever you announce a policy or a decision, describe the thought process behind it, along with relevant facts and figures. As was the case with my son, even if your employees don't agree, they'll respect your decision more if you explain your reasoning.

10. Prepare them for the unexpected. One way to prepare your people to deal with uncertainty is to anticipate every possible scenario and rehearse the most effective responses. That's how soldiers, athletes, and others who perform in unpredictable conditions are trained, and businesses can do the same. So, while training your employees for ordinary tasks, make sure you also prepare them for every unusual situation that might crop up and train them to handle each contingency. You'll never think of everything, but you should be able to anticipate most potential challenges.

At Walt Disney World, Cast Members had to be prepared for all kinds of circumstances—not just major upheavals like hurricanes but minor hassles like a child getting sick on a ride and a Guest losing a wallet. One strategy we used to anticipate these was to have every manager write down all the surprises that tended to crop up in his or her line of work. By drawing from their own experiences, managers usually came up with quite a comprehensive list. Then we'd have a team of managers and frontline Cast Members create operating guidelines for handling each situation. For example, "When a Guest loses his park ticket, take him immediately to guest services so it can check the records and replace the ticket" or "If a Guest gets upset because the restaurant ran out of her favorite dish, apologize and offer her a complementary entrée."

If you and your employees put your minds to it, you should be able to anticipate most difficult situations. Once you have response guidelines in place, you can even use techniques like role playing and dress rehearsals to train your people in the proper responses.

Bill Marriott once told me something I never forgot: "Lee, the only way you get excellence in anything is with education and enforcement." I would update Mr. Marriott's statement to say, "The only way you achieve excellence is with education, enforcement, and large doses of recognition, appreciation, and encouragement" (the subject of Chapter Nine).

Remember, if you don't train and develop your employees, you'll lose them to a company that will. Recently a young friend of mine named Casey resigned from his organization, even though he was highly valued and was being promoted ahead of his peers. I asked Casey why he would give up a promising future at age twenty-nine. His answer should be a wake-up call for all organizations. "I was trained really, really well," he said, "but I was never developed. No one took the time to get to know me, coach me, counsel me, or even ask me what my aspirations were. I have a lot of weaknesses, I'm sure, but no one ever discussed them with me. It was all about getting the job done for them and nothing about me and my personal development." He has just been snapped up by a major company and is already being groomed for higher leadership responsibility.

Managers often ask me how much time they should spend training and developing their employees. My answer is always the same: "A lot." There are no formulas for this and no hard data that point to an ideal number of hours per week. But I can say this: If you have to ask whether you're doing enough to train and develop your people, the answer is you're probably not. Ask yourself the following questions on a regular basis, and see if you're satisfied with your answers.

* Do the people who work for you act as though they just have a job, or do they perform with a sense of purpose?

* Can every employee explain your organization's vision or purpose?

* How easy do you make it for employees to access opportunities to learn?

* How many people have been developed and promoted under your leadership?

* How many classes, courses, or seminars does your company offer? How many do you personally conduct?

* How often do experts from inside or outside your organization share their knowledge with your employees?

* What are your results on measures of customer and employee satisfaction?

* Have those results improved steadily or declined?

* How does your organization stack up on performance indicators?

Remember, great teachers usually make great leaders. So make it a priority to give everyone who works for you the tools, coaching, and sense of purpose he or she needs to be the very best. After all, that's what making Disney magic is all about.

ACTION STEPS

* Make sure every employee is fully steeped in your corporate culture.

* Create clear statements of your values and mission, and see to it that everyone understands their meaning.

* Inculcate a sense of purpose in everyone at every level of your organization.

* Take seriously your responsibilities as a teacher, coach, and counselor.

* Teach your employees how to perform the technical aspects of their roles *and* how to exceed customers' expectations.

* Train people to do your equivalent of Take 5s and Magic Moments.

* Explain clearly the key drivers of customer satisfaction for each person's role.

✳ Create multiple ways to communicate regularly with your staff.

✳ Give constructive feedback promptly and effectively.

✳ Make sure everyone understands what's expected of him or her.

✳ Conduct periodic tests of knowledge and skills.

✳ Remember, you're teaching by example every minute of every day.

CHAPTER SEVEN

STRATEGY #5

ELIMINATE HASSLES

O ne morning, a few weeks into my tenure as general manager of the Marriott in Springfield, Massachusetts, an irate guest came to my office. The night before, he and his wife had come to the hotel restaurant to celebrate their twenty-fifth wedding anniversary. They ordered two lobster dinners and an expensive bottle of Chardonnay. Then they waited for the wine . . . and waited . . . and waited some more. Soon the lobsters arrived, but still not the wine. By the time they could toast their marriage, all that remained on their plates were lobster shells. What should have been a special occasion had been tainted by irritation and frustration. I apologized and invited the couple to come back and reenact their anniversary celebration on the house.

That night, at the pre-shift meeting at the restaurant, I asked the servers to describe the process for serving wine. They told me that when a guest ordered a bottle, the server first had to ring up the price on the guest check, then show the check to the restaurant manager, who would open the securely locked wine cabinet and retrieve the correct bottle. That wine cabinet was actually in the dining room, but the manager was the only person allowed to have a key.

The server who had waited on the anniversary couple explained that he had not been able to locate the manager for nearly half an hour. It seems that the manager was doing something in the storeroom and hadn't told anyone where he was going. And since he was the only one with a key to the wine cabinet, the couple did not get their wine until they were ready to order dessert.

"OK," I said, "let me explain the *new* process to you. From now on, when we open the restaurant each night, the manager will unlock the wine cabinet. When a guest orders a bottle of wine, the server will ring it up on the check, get the wine, and serve it. At the end of the night the manager will balance the wine cabinet stock with the wine orders and relock the cabinet. Also, the manager will from time to time, at random, ask to see the servers' open checks. Serving wine to a guest before ringing it up will be considered a serious matter, and there will be consequences."

We never had a repeat of the anniversary mishap. Even better, we sold a lot more wine because guests were now served so promptly they had time to order a second bottle with their meal. In fact, everyone was happy: The customers got their wine promptly, the servers' tips went up, and the manager had fewer complaints and hassles to contend with.

So far we have discussed how to create an effective organizational structure, put the right people in the right roles, and train and develop them within the context of an inclusive, creative culture. But even well-trained people in a great environment can't create magic if they don't have sound processes for getting the work done right. Every business is run by processes.

Whether they're called rules, procedures, policies, or operating guidelines, processes define how employees should interact with other people—coworkers, customers, and external business contacts—as well as with the physical environment and technology in order to accomplish specific tasks in the best and most efficient way. Effective processes make the routine things run smoothly and consistently, freeing employees to do the extra things that can turn a good business into a great business. Ineffective processes, on the other hand, create chaos, confusion, and hassles. And hassles lead to alienated customers and frustrated employees. They can turn a good business into a losing or even a failed one.

Think about it. We get to work reliably because of processes that regulate traffic and make the trains run on time. Our kids advance from one grade to another because schools have processes for teaching, grading, and promoting students. There's even a process for putting the trash out, including exactly what goes in the recycle bin and what can and can't be put out on certain days. But we rarely think about such processes until they break down. Just think about the last time you got stranded in an airport because a storm interfered with the usual processes for air travel or a labor dispute caused the garbage to pile up or the public transportation system to stop running.

What I said about organizational structure in Chapter Four applies equally to processes: You ignore the details at your peril. If you really want to maximize the potential of your employees and the satisfaction of your customers, the last thing you want is to subject them to hassles caused by bad procedures. One of your responsibilities as a leader therefore is to identify process problems and act as quickly as possible to fix them.

Some leaders think evaluating processes is too boring, too

technical, or too mundane for creative visionaries like them to bother with. But no less a creative visionary than Walt Disney understood the power of process and made it a central feature of the company he built. As his business grew from one young genius working in a garage to teams of artists, writers, composers, and technicians making animated movies, he invented the processes that made his on-screen magic possible. Then, when he opened Disneyland, he created processes for everything from the timing of a theme park ride to the serving of a hot dog, all designed to keep the place humming and blow the minds of Guests with excellent service. And Walt didn't wait for employees and customers to complain about hassles before he re-evaluated his processes. As a great leader always should, he *looked* for ways to improve how things are done because "We've always done it that way" could mean that you've been doing it wrong all along. In fact, the wine bottle process that caused the anniversary disaster had been in place for many years. The restaurant manager, and others before him, had just accepted it, instead of questioning it and taking on the responsibility of improving it.

One reason Walt Disney loved his theme parks was that unlike the films he made, a park was never finished. He could constantly find better ways of doing things. "I want something live," he once said, "something that would grow. The park is that. Not only can I add things, but even the trees will keep growing. The thing will get more beautiful year after year." That's your job as a leader: to help your business grow by paying attention to your employees and your customers and by constantly fine-tuning your processes—within appropriate limits of cost and safety, of course—so that every job gets done efficiently and without hassles. The following tips will help you do that.

1. Ask what rather than who. When that restaurant guest told me about his unfortunate anniversary dinner, my first reaction could have been to reprimand the server or penalize the manager. Fortunately, I had already learned an important leadership lesson: When a mishap arises, instead of immediately looking for someone to blame, first see if a flawed procedure or policy is causing the problem.

Ruling out process snags first is a more efficient way to respond, and it makes a huge difference in morale. Discipline is necessary only when someone intentionally ignores procedures, but if the procedures themselves are flawed, blaming can be destructive. So when complaint patterns emerge, make it your default position to backtrack through the system to find out the causes—not the who but the what. More often than you might suspect the glitch will turn out to be procedural.

2. Listen to your customers. Most complaints businesses receive from customers point to process failures. If you read their letters and e-mails with that in mind, you gain invaluable information about what types of process changes you should be working on.

One Saturday morning, while shopping at Costco, I bought my wife a new suitcase for a trip to Europe. But when I brought it home, Priscilla said it wasn't big enough, so I went back and returned it for a full refund, no questions asked. From the time I walked into the store until the time I was back in my car, less than five minutes had passed. On another occasion I tried to return a sink faucet at a large chain store (which I won't name). The man in the plumbing department pummeled me with questions: Why was I unhappy with the faucet? Did it not work properly? What was wrong with it? And so on. Once he was satisfied I had a good reason to return the faucet, he said he had to get a manager's approval. Only no one with the authority to approve returns was available. It was more than an hour before I got to see the general manager, who finally approved the return. Do I have to tell you that I never went back to that store? Or that I am a loyal customer at Costco?

Point is, people are in a hurry these days, so speeding up processes should be a constant goal of any business. This is especially true of processes that can be annoying and time-consuming, like returning merchandise, calling customer service, and checking out with your purchases. I was recently at a new Wal-Mart store, for instance, and I saw that low pricing is not the only reason the company is so successful. Not only do its processes keep its shelves well stocked, but the checkout system, including credit card approval, is lightning quick; plus the stores are clean and the employees are friendly. At theme parks like *Walt Disney World*® Resort, of course, the leading cause of complaints is waiting in line. Over the years the company has been relentless in trying to shorten queue times for popular attractions and to make the waiting period as pleasant and as comfortable as possible. Cast Members are trained to treat impatient Guests with kindness and to keep restless children occupied; video screens are displayed to entertain and inform the people in line. And in 1999 a major innovation was introduced: a computerized reservation process called FAST-PASS® that enables Guests to sign up, with a quick swipe of their admission passes, for a one-hour time slot at an attraction later that day; when they return during their allotted hour, they move rapidly to the attraction in a special line.

The FASTPASS® was a great solution to a perpetual challenge that many had considered insurmountable. Just goes to show that sometimes, with a little insight and creativity, you can make process changes that no one would even expect but that make a huge difference to grateful customers. Not long ago Walt Disney World introduced a process, called *Disney's Magical Express*, that made checking out of its hotels and getting to the airport a breeze. Cast Members had seen so many harried parents trying to corral rambunctious kids and keep track of carry-on bags, loose tickets, and luggage that they found a way to make the process of moving from lobby to airport terminal easier. Now Guests can check their luggage and get their boarding passes at their hotels before they check out and take a Disney coach straight to the airport. As you can imagine, eliminating those hassles gave the company yet another competitive advantage.

Here's another one. For years Guests had a limited number of choices regarding the kind of admission ticket they could buy. But they told us, through focus groups, letters, surveys, and complaints at the ticket desks, that they wanted more options. So we added some. For instance, we adjusted the Park Hopper ticket, which admitted Guests to any of the four parks within a three-day period, to include one- and two-day versions. In fact, Guests can now have pretty much any combination of options they want if they're willing to pay for them, and many of them are.

3. Learn firsthand what's working and what's not. At a hotel I once managed, arriving guests sometimes complained that amenities they'd requested, like a crib or refrigerator, were not in their rooms. After hearing one too many irritated moms and dads yelling at the desk manager while their babies shrieked in the background, I decided to look into the situation. To my dismay, I discovered that we had lousy systems for meeting such requests. So I introduced a system by which guests were asked when they made their reservations what time they expected to arrive, so the housekeepers could fill special requests well in advance. Later on we took the process a step further. We kept track of which items were requested most frequently and placed some of them permanently in the rooms. The cost of adding irons, ironing boards, coffeemakers, extra pillows, and refrigerators was more than offset by the increase in guest satisfaction and the reduction in labor cost that came from not needing extra staff to deliver popular items when someone asked for them. It also meant never having to apologize to an upset guest because a requested item was missing.

That chain of process improvements might never have gotten off the ground if I hadn't heard the complaints firsthand. From then on I made it a point to listen to feedback personally and take charge of getting the process fixed instead of delegating it further down the chain of command. Remember that couple whose anniversary was ruined by the late-arriving wine? The reason I learned about it so quickly was that I had already established a process that enabled disgruntled guests to come straight to me. Pasted on the front of every menu was a two-inch-high gold sticker that read, "If you are not happy with any part of your experience in this restaurant, please contact the restaurant manager or me," with my name and title. The fast, personal response from someone in a leadership position made all the difference between customer loyalty and customer loss.

At Walt Disney World we used to write letters of apology to Guests who complained. But these apologies seemed to fall on deaf ears. So we started *phoning* those Guests instead. Sure, phone calls take a lot more time than writing letters and e-mails. But the two-way conversations enabled us to understand fully the nature of every person's complaint. Plus think of what it meant to unhappy Guests to hear from a polite, caring person who wanted to find out the details and find a way to make it up to them. I don't think we can calculate the number of process changes we made that we might never have thought of without those one-on-one conversations—or how much money the company earned because Guests who might not have returned, or might not have recommended Disney World to others, had a change of heart thanks to those phone calls.

4. Constantly query employees. As a leader you have to keep your ear to the ground and listen for the sound of complaints from your staff. It helps to have a process in place to root out process problems and then follow up to make sure they're resolved.

When I became general manager of a Marriott hotel, I set up an advisory group of frontline employees from every department and met with them once a week for an hour. Also present were the director of human resources and the director of maintenance, since most of the problems that came up related to those two areas. My secretary wrote down everything that was said, from complaints about a leaky faucet to broken vacuum cleaners to equipment shortages to safety concerns, and on and on. We sent the list to the relevant department heads so they could fix the problems, preferably before the next meeting, when we reviewed each item to see if it had been resolved. Every item was numbered, and it stayed on the list until it was satisfactorily addressed.

This process not only made sure that nothing slipped through the cracks but also trained people at every level to continuously evaluate their processes and never to accept "This is the way it's done" as the final answer. We got them in the habit of asking questions like "Why do we do it that way?," "What would happen if we didn't have this procedure?," and "What's the risk of changing it?" The process also played a major role in building trust. We posted the list of concerns on every bulletin board, so employees knew I was listening to them and taking care of the issues they cared about. And when they saw that management was serious about tackling the problems, they were even more willing to tell us about them.

Remember, if you don't follow up, your credibility is zero, and people will clam up. Some concerns might seem insignificant to you, but they can be very important to your employees. Among the problems you'll hear about if you pay attention are internal matters like cumbersome processes for putting in for vacation time or clocking in and out. Others can wreak havoc on an individual's family: hassles in correcting an error in a paycheck, for instance, or requesting a schedule change in an emergency. Other kinks in the process are more systemic and costly—like how to calculate the payroll, or pay suppliers on time, or collect delinquent accounts receivable.

Here is an example of a process change from Disney World that made employees' lives easier and also saved the company money. At one point we required Cast Members to go to the costuming department every day to exchange their worn costumes for fresh ones. We kept hearing Cast Members say what a hassle it was, so we changed the process to allow them to check out as many as five costumes at once and either wash them at home or exchange all five at a time. Cast Members saved time because they didn't have to go to costuming every day, and the company saved money in cleaning costs.

So, train your employees to identify process problems, but don't just wait for them to come to you. Gather appropriate groups for process discussions. At Disney I held regular meetings to stimulate team thinking about processes, policies, rules, and operating guidelines. I called them stop/start/continue discussions because we asked ourselves which processes should be stopped, which new ones should be started, and which existing ones should be continued. For instance, one process we decided to stop was requiring Guests to sign charge card receipts for purchases under twenty-five dollars. The change sped up the transaction time at the point of sale without appreciably increasing the risk of fraud. One process we decided to start was asking Guests for photo IDs when they checked in, a security precaution instituted after 9/11. And a process that we decided to continue was to have pre-shift meetings every day for each department. After careful discussion, we determined that this was a useful practice, and so the proposed alternative, holding meetings only a couple of times a week to save managers' time, was rejected.

Sometimes changing a process requires a combination of starts, stops, and continuations. For example, in a discussion about how to cut down on lost and broken dishware: "Let's *stop* counting the dishware daily and *start* counting it once a week, and let's *continue* to train the kitchen staff to stack the dishes properly so we don't break as many."

Direct reports also used this model to give feedback about what they would like their bosses to stop doing, start doing, and continue doing. For example, a manager might hear, "We would like you to *stop* calling meetings so often without giving us notice, because it's causing us to fall behind in our work. We would like you to *start* using an agenda for our meetings to keep them on track and focused. And we would like to see you *continue* meeting with us once a month to discuss our performance and to get to know us better."

5. Harvest process solutions from employees. This could be the most important tip in this chapter. Your employees are not just ideally placed to identify process problems but also well suited to solving them. They are, after all, the ones who do the work and interact with customers.

If I described every great idea that Disney Cast Members contribute in just one year, it would take up the entire book. But here are a few. At one time the hotel housekeepers were frustrated with how long it took, and how tiring it was, to push their carts around on the thick hallway carpets. So they asked if the company could provide motorized carts. It turned out to be a great investment: The housekeepers get more done in less time and with less strain on their bodies, and the company saves a bundle of money thanks to reduced absenteeism and medical costs. Another time the parking lot attendants came up with an ingenious solution to the perpetual problem of Guests' being unable to find their cars after a long day of entertainment. Each attendant now has a diagram of the vast parking lot. Systematically, the attendants note what time each section fills up. When Guests can't remember where they parked, they're asked, "What time did you arrive?" This narrows down the possible locations tremendously, and the Guests are taken in golf carts to find their cars.

Here's another story I love to tell, from Disney's Textile Services. In the last chapter I told you the story of the knot in the ironing tape. Well, the process actually begins when big carts arrive at a dock holding a few hundred pounds of dirty sheets, pillowcases, and towels, where Cast Members dump the goods onto a conveyor belt to begin the trip through washing, drying, and ironing. At one point, tired of climbing into the carts to pick up linen that got stuck in the corners, the Cast Members jerry-rigged a tool for themselves by bending a thick piece of wire into the shape of a hook and wrapping tape around it. That extended their reach by two or three feet, enabling them to reach into the corners.

That improvement was itself improved a few years later, when a manager asked the Cast Members to come up with some money-saving ideas. One of the cart dumpers pointed out that the self-made hooks had been tearing a lot of sheets, and the torn sheets were either thrown out or ended up inadvertently on a Guest's bed. The manager asked him how they might solve the problem. "Make it round instead of pointed," was the reply. So machinists took a blowtorch to the hooks and made them blunt. Ken Miratsky, the manager of housekeeping laundry, calculates that the improved hook has saved the company about $120,000 a year in torn sheets.

To reiterate a point I've made several times, *every* company can learn from examples like these. When leaders at Florida-based Mercedes Homes heard the parking lot story at a Disney Institute training program, they were inspired to ask their frontline people what issues needed to be resolved and how best to resolve them. One employee mentioned that many of the older people for whom the company built houses did not have the physical ability to install shutters when a hurricane was expected. As a result, their houses suffered greater damage than others. Another employee came up with a process solution: Keep a file of elderly home buyers, and when a storm is expected, have representatives contact them to see if they need help. A simple, elegant service that saved a number of houses—and was great for customer relations.

6. Try an audit exchange plan. Here's another strategy I recommend to help employees identify and solve process problems. At both Marriott and Walt Disney World I added a system called an audit exchange, in which managers of different resorts or parks spend a day auditing the operations of their peers. On the premise that it is easier to see with fresh eyes when we're outside our usual frame of reference, we told the resort and park managers to look for weaknesses in one another's controls, costs, and procedures. They spent the day visiting different departments, asking questions of the department managers and frontline staff, and observing operations. The results were excellent: Not only did the managers spot flaws in the operations they visited, but they also found good ideas for processes and procedures to implement in their own departments.

Once, when one of our general managers at Disney audited a colleague's hotel, he was surprised to find animal keepers from Disney's Animal Kingdom in the lobby, giving talks and demonstrations about small birds and animals, making the time go by more quickly and enjoyably for Guests who had to wait in long check-in lines. The GM went back to his own hotel and started providing similar entertainment on busy check-in days. Another manager auditing a hotel saw a special check-in line for return Guests. While first-time Guests usually need explanations about the packages they purchase, returning Guests do not, so having separate lines sped up the process for *everyone*. The manager then instituted a similar process at her hotel.

7. Stay technically up-to-date. Advances in computers and other technologies have made it possible to speed up processes, cut costs, and eliminate hassles like never before. At Disney, for example, we've taken advantage of all kinds of new technologies that have emerged over the years. It was once common for hotel Guests to return to their rooms late in the day only to find that they had not yet been made up. As we reviewed the problem, we realized that our own management process was flawed; managers had no system for tracking which rooms had been made up. So we implemented a new electronic system: Housekeepers punch a code into the room's telephone when they've completed cleaning it; the codes are then transmitted to a computer database; managers access the information from their offices and other locations and learn exactly which rooms have been made up and which have not. Then they can inform the housekeepers to ensure that every room is done by 3:00 P.M.

This long-standing process problem was solved because someone was up-to-date with punch code technology. Leaders who do not keep up with technology are doing themselves and their companies a great disservice. This doesn't require becoming a geek (although it might mean *hiring* some geeks) or spending large amounts of time doing research. Just look around you. Does a computerized voice in your new car tell you when to bring it in for servicing? Maybe you can apply a technology like that in your business. Can you access your children's grades online? Maybe you can put some information online to eliminate hassles in your workplace. At Disney, for instance, employees can log on to the Internet at home and access their schedules, update their personal information, check on their benefits or vacation time, and do all sorts of things that used to require a phone call or a visit to an office.

Here's another example of how we took advantage of computer technology to solve a process problem at Disney. We used to find people who wanted to work overtime the old-fashioned way, by asking around. As you can imagine, this was a cumbersome, inefficient process, and managers complained that they wasted a lot of time hunting down willing workers. So we took advantage of the Disney Intranet service and set up a special

Web site where Cast Members can sign up for an overtime assignment anywhere on the property. This made all overtime available to every Cast Member on a first-come, first-served basis. We never again had a problem filling overtime slots.

In addition to keeping up with technological advances, it's important to stay on top of relevant industry-related research— or even conduct it yourself. One of the compliments Disney World has received for decades is that the parks are amazingly spotless. When you consider how many kids tromp through the place and how much eating and snacking are done, the cleanliness is a remarkable achievement. How do we do it? It's not just that the trash is removed like clockwork and that Cast Members are trained to pick up litter whenever they see it. Next time you walk up Main Street in the Magic Kingdom or some other thoroughfare in one of the parks, count off the number of steps between the trash containers. You'll find that they're spaced about twenty-five paces apart. This isn't arbitrary; it was based on a study that determined both the length of time it takes to remove a candy wrapper and the average distance a Guest could walk in that time. Those data helped us design the best trash container layout for the grounds and have made a huge difference in preserving the cleanliness and overall appearance of the parks.

8. Think ahead. Don't just wait for hassles to appear; find ways to prevent them before they happen. Remember the old navy saying "For every regulation, there's a dead sailor." It means that nothing changes unless someone falls overboard. As I said in the previous chapter, it's vital for leaders to anticipate problems and prepare their employees to handle them. Part of the credit for Disney World's outstanding response to the 2004 hurricanes goes to the intricate processes that were put into place beforehand. Every detail was worked out in advance, from having box lunches ready to hand out to Guests to placing entertainers in the hotels to stave off boredom until it was safe to go outdoors to preparing to clear fallen trees off the roads when the worst was over. And we adjusted with each lesson learned. When we discovered that many Cast Members could not come to the property to help out during storms because they didn't want to leave their pets at home, we added something to the process: kennels.

Above all, we had established procedures for simulating emergency situations. Once or twice a year an outside company came to the property to simulate and run through various emergency situations—not just hurricanes but other disasters like a chlorine spill, a chemical attack, and so on—as realistically as possible. When the real thing hit, those rigorous rehearsals paid major dividends.

9. Look at your personal processes. Many leaders stay on top of the systems their employees use but ignore their own. Some resist having anything resembling a routine; they think it's boring, and they want to remain fluid and flexible to respond to changing circumstances. But good routines actually give you the stability you need in order to adapt when challenges arise. I once heard someone say, "Management is boring. If you want excitement become a race car driver." His point was that good managers aren't there to seek thrills; they are there to keep things under control, minimize the unexpected disruptions, and give their employees the consistency they need to do their best work. Good processes ensure that you attend to the routine, necessary, and predictable tasks, freeing your mind to respond creatively to unexpected events.

Being poorly organized is one of the biggest problems leaders run into, and they don't always recognize it. Crises keep erupting around them, and they don't realize that many could have been averted if they'd been better organized in the first place. And the more fires they have to put out, the more they resist getting organized, because they can't stop long enough to take stock of their routines.

I was like that myself once. When I was regional director of food and beverage operations for Marriott, I received a memo from my boss telling me that I had to attend a time management seminar. I said, "I don't have time to go to a two-day seminar on time management." I thought I was already well organized. I may have been working far too many nights and weekends, but I always got my work done on time, and I consistently earned a great performance rating. It took awhile, but I eventually learned that the people who don't have the time to learn time management are the ones who need it the most, as I did. What I learned in that seminar has been central to everything I've accomplished since.

Among other things, I learned how to set priorities as opposed to trying to do everything. I learned how to involve other people and delegate tasks instead of doing it all myself. I learned to lead one full life instead of trying to lead two separate ones—one business and one personal. I learned to enter personal necessities—time with family and friends, my daily workouts, etc.—as appointments on my calendar, just like business meetings. No question about it, improving my personal processes helped me eliminate hassles, both personal and professional, at every turn. And it helped make me a better leader to boot. As you can see, management and leadership are closely connected. Managerial skills give you credibility; unless you are organized, do what you say you are going to do, and keep your promises, you will not be considered a great leader.

So step back periodically and evaluate your organizing processes—and not just during your working hours. Make sure your whole life is under control, or else the personal and professional will spill into each other and create a mess on both ends. You might want to take a course in time management or perhaps hire a coach to help you create a personal system. Get yourself a digital organizer or an old-fashioned paper version, or both. As I mentioned earlier, I've been using a Day-Timer for many years, and I also have a BlackBerry; the three of us complement one another really well. Whatever system you select, get it up and running as soon as possible, and keep it with you 24/7. (Day-Timer offers a very good time management course. For information, go to its Web site, www.daytimer.com.) Here are some additional organizing tips I've found to be useful.

√ Take five to thirty minutes each morning to plan your day.

√ Use that time to list all the things you need to get done or get started on that day.

√ In making that list, ask yourself these three questions:

- Of all of the responsibilities I have signed up for in my life, which ones should I work on today?

- What should I start today that will not pay off for one, five, ten, twenty, or even forty years from now?

- What did I do yesterday that I need to go back and do better?

Time has a way of getting away from busy people. So if you think that being organized is only for uncreative drones, think again. The time you save by being organized is time you can spend learning new things, thinking up new ideas, or implementing innovations. Positive routines create positive outcomes, period.

10. Expect resistance. As with an established structure, when you change an established process, be prepared for opposition. As I say in Chapter Four, it's important to listen carefully to all the arguments before making a decision. Remember, someone put the current process into place for a reason. That reason may have made perfect sense at the time—and in fact, it still might—but if you determine that it needs to be altered or eliminated, you have to work through the resistance skillfully. Of course this takes courage, and you can't make significant improvements without that.

When I came to Orlando from Paris, I suggested a process change that drew a lot of resistance from the Cast. I'd noticed that many hotels in Europe did not change the bed sheets every day (of course, if a guest stayed only one night, the sheets were changed before the next guest arrived). The idea was to conserve water and cut down on labor costs, and it seemed pretty smart to me. But when I suggested it at Disney World, I was almost run out of town. "Great hotels *always* change the sheets every day," I was told. "Only fleabag hotels wouldn't." It was assumed that our Guests would vote against such a change with their feet. But I had faith in the idea, and since it was a reversible decision, I said to the resisters, "Why don't we try it in one hotel and see what happens? If it doesn't work, we'll go back to changing the sheets every day."

We tested the concept at the two-thousand-room Caribbean Beach Resort. A written statement was placed in every room explaining that the new policy would save millions of gallons of water a day and keep tons of chemicals from entering the environment. We told Guests we'd be happy to accommodate anyone who wanted his or her sheets changed daily, and we recorded those requests in our housekeeping system. We also trained our housekeepers to change any linen that had been stained. The naysayers were shocked. On an average day, only one or two Guests requested a sheet change, and many sent letters complimenting us for caring about the environment. When we took the experiment to other resorts, we got the same positive response. Pretty soon even those who originally thought I was crazy came around. I've never been happier that I stuck to my guns. We achieved major savings on labor because the housekeepers could now clean more rooms in less time, and we also saved on detergents and other cleaning expenses. We even canceled the planned purchase of a new washer that would have cost a million dollars.

One important way to work through resistance is to get support for your ideas from frontline employees. A few years ago the management at Disney's Textile Services wanted to increase the number of items it moved through the operation each day. It discovered a machine that would bump the rate of productivity from 800 items per hour to 1,000. That's such a big process improvement that the machine would pay for itself in a matter of months. But management knew that Cast Members would resist out of fear that the automation would cost some of them their jobs. So before purchasing the machine, the leaders held a series of meetings with the Cast. They showed videos, explained the financials, and invited feedback. Because the Cast Members whose lives would be impacted by the change felt included in the decision-making process (and were assured that no jobs would be lost—those who counted on overtime were reallocated to areas that had extra work), they enthusiastically endorsed the plan. As soon as the machine was installed, the department started processing 25,600 more pillowcases per day. In the subsequent years, as the resorts grew and more and more linen had to be processed, the savings to the company have been immense.

It is your responsibility as a leader to constantly look for and implement new and better processes in your business operations and to work hard to gain support for those initiatives.

Now for the inevitable caveat: Some process changes seem to make a great deal of sense but still should not be made. Sometimes you have to sacrifice efficiency for safety and security. Keeping cash in a secure safe or password-protecting the company computers might cause hassles, but securing your equipment, cash, and property and keeping your employees and customers safe always take precedence over speed and convenience.

11. Periodically evaluate the changes you make. Remember the old adage "Don't expect if you don't inspect." Introducing new processes is easy; the hard part is getting them to stick. So before you implement new procedures, take the time to communicate thoroughly with everyone who will be affected by them. Explain exactly *why* the change is important to employees, customers, or business results. As I mentioned earlier, if you have a good explanation for your decision, people will be more likely to get on board with it. And once the change is made, it's your job to ensure that what's put into place *stays* in place. I strongly suggest walking through your operation day after day to check on all the processes and systems. Don't just ask how it's going; check on it yourself.

As with structural innovations, it's crucial to avoid falling in love with your brilliant process changes. So make every adjustment with the attitude that it's reversible, that not only *can* you change it again, but you eventually will have to. Also keep in mind that eliminating or altering a process might cause problems you never anticipated. At Disney it was often a hassle for customers to return merchandise if they did not have receipts, so we started letting them make returns without one. Then we discovered that some people were walking into our stores, picking up goods, and bringing them to the registers for refunds. So we changed the process back to requiring receipts, and we trained managers to make appropriate exceptions for Guests who had lost theirs.

Keep in mind that a process can make sense in one environment but not in another. In 2006, Wal-Mart implemented a policy to no longer prosecute shoplifters for lifting goods that cost less than three dollars. It simply was not worth the cost. At one time Disney World had a similarly lenient policy. But in the mid-nineties the word got out that shoplifters were let go when caught, so local schoolkids started having contests over who could steal the most. And it wasn't just kids. Dishonest employees, parents, and even grandparents were pilfering prized souvenirs from the gift shops. It was estimated that we were losing as much as 3 percent of total sales. So we changed the process. Now every theft is prosecuted, and security has been beefed up by hidden cameras and by adding security personnel dressed as ordinary Guests.

Always approach a process change as an experiment. Try out new processes for thirty to ninety days; then follow up systematically to see if they've been implemented as you envisioned and have genuinely taken hold, or if things have reverted to the way they were before or otherwise gone awry. When it comes to innovation, it's important to remember the Chinese injunction to be like bamboo: firm and strong but also flexible enough to bend with the winds of change.

ACTION STEPS

✳ When a problem arises, seek out the process failure; don't just look for someone to blame.

✳ Continually identify customer and employee hassles, and change your processes to make the hassles go away.

✳ Ask the frontline employees to identify process obstacles that interfere with satisfying customers or getting their jobs done.

✳ Ask your customers what processes cause difficulties for them and what they like and don't like about your business procedures.

✳ Call some of your unhappy customers yourself to learn firsthand the details of the process problem.

✳ Keep your processes up-to-date with the latest technology and relevant research.

✳ Make sure you have processes in place to prepare for problems before they arise.

✳ Eliminate headaches from your personal routine by getting organized.

✳ Check new processes three to six months later to see if they have taken hold.

✳ Ask, "Why do we do it that way?" more often.

✳ Explore how process changes might give you more time for coaching, counseling, and training your employees.

* Look for process changes that would give your managers more time to spend with customers.

* Ask yourself, "How many ideas and suggestions for process improvements have I generated and tracked in the last thirty days?"

* Always examine how well employees understand and support the processes and operating guidelines you currently have in place.

CHAPTER EIGHT

STRATEGY #6

LEARN THE TRUTH

As the detective Joe Friday from the old *Dragnet* TV series would say, "Just the facts, ma'am." That's what leaders need: the facts. If you don't know the facts, how can you possibly make the best decisions? Just read the newspaper any day of the week, and you'll see the results of regrettable decisions made by leaders who acted on flawed or incomplete information.

Great leaders are always in a learning mode. To them, truth is more precious than gold; they know that the more of it they have, the more successful they'll be. So they constantly explore and probe, listen to everyone, and utilize all reasonable methods for gathering information. Yes, ferreting out the facts is time-consuming, but would you rather invest that time now and make smart, well-informed decisions or put in even more time on the back end, correcting mistakes, replacing good people who quit in frustration, or scrambling to catch up to competitors who surged ahead in market share? Even worse, would you prefer to spend time and resources dealing with a legal or financial disaster that catches you by surprise? Remember, "I had no idea that was going on" is not an acceptable explanation for a leader. As we've all seen, more than a few corporate executives have sought in vain to defend themselves by claiming ignorance of their operations. Knowing what's going on is your responsibility, and if something goes seriously wrong, you'll always wish you'd had the information to prevent it.

Can you ever know everything? No. Can you always learn more? Of course you can. That's your job. If you don't do all you can to dig out the truth every chance you get, you risk making bad decisions. I've seen it happen to a great many otherwise competent leaders. Some rely too much on vague data and dubious information; some isolate themselves, acting as though employees below a certain level had nothing to offer; some get defensive in the face of constructive criticism; and some develop reputations for lashing out at those who deliver unpleasant facts, so people stop coming to them with candid information.

No matter what kind of work you do, if you aspire to truly great leadership, you need to get all the facts pertaining to your business or operation. As Fox Mulder, a modern-day Joe Friday from *The X-Files*, would say, "The truth is out there." The following tips will help you find it.

1. Get out and about routinely. Even though he was busy running one of the world's biggest entertainment empires, Walt Disney used to spend a great deal of time walking around Disneyland, speaking to Guests and Cast Members. And he made sure his executives and managers did the same. In fact, the offices in Anaheim had no air conditioning in those days because Walt wanted people out in the park, learning about the operation firsthand rather than being cool and comfortable but out of touch. Once a week, company leaders were expected to get a

Guest-eye's view; they'd park their cars in the Guest lot, eat where the Guests ate, stand in line to ride the attractions, and so on. A long list of innovations and improvements grew directly from those close encounters with the Guest experience, from how to organize queues, to the onstage-backstage concept so central to the magic of *Walt Disney World*® Resort. One day, while out and about in the Anaheim park, Walt was distressed to see a cowboy from Frontierland walk through the futuristic landscape of Tomorrowland. Concerned that such incongruous sights could destroy the sense of magic, he later designed the Magic Kingdom with a network of arteries fourteen feet belowground so that all backstage functions, from offices to deliveries to Cast parking lots to garbage removal, are completely out of sight, and Cast Members can move from place to place undetected.

I had come to see the value of getting out and about and learning the facts firsthand before I even came to Disney; maybe that's one of the reasons why I was such a good fit. When I ran the Springfield Marriott, for example, I spent more time roaming the building than I did in my office. I'd arrive at 6:00 every morning and check out the lobby, the three public elevators, the driveway (you'd be surprised what you find in elevators and driveways first thing in the morning, and believe me, they're usually things you don't want your guests to see), and even the mailbox on the corner to make sure they all were clean. I'd walk from floor to floor to check out the stairwells, and I'd roam the corridors of all fourteen floors to make certain there were no room service trays with dirty dishes and nasty-looking leftovers lingering outside the doors. I'd check out the banquet rooms, conference rooms, and storerooms; the restaurants, kitchens, and walk-in coolers; the public bathrooms; the receiving dock and Dumpsters; and even the employee cafeteria and locker rooms because I wanted staff members to know I cared about their facilities as well. Along the way I'd stop to chat with workers and managers, thanking them for doing a good job and asking what they thought needed my attention. When I spotted something wrong, I'd make a note of it in my Day-Timer for follow-up.

By 7:00 I'd be in my office with a full set of notes to review with my executive committee. Everyone on the committee knew that in twenty-four hours I would be taking that exact walk again, and that any problems I noted—especially safety issues—should be addressed by then. And they almost always were. It wasn't long, for instance, before I stopped seeing room service trays in the hallways; knowing my routine, the staff started clearing them away regularly—once at midnight and then again at 5:45 A.M.

I'd make personal trips to key locations regularly throughout each day, and I'd make the full tour again before I went home. Getting out and about regularly was a great investment of time. Not only did it allow me to see the operations up close, but it helped me get to know everyone on the staff better, and all of them in turn became more comfortable telling me what I needed to know.

I kept up that tradition in every position I had, and I made sure other leaders followed suit. "Walk Cast and Guest areas several times a day" was a key principle I emphasized at Disney World. I urge you to do the same, especially when you first arrive at work each day. It will enable you to root out flaws, measure progress, and resolve minor problems before they become major issues. Be visible in the work areas and in the break rooms, and talk to people as you make your rounds. Ask if anything is standing in the way of great performance, whether it's sluggish procedures, unclear operating guidelines, obsolete equipment, inadequate training, etc. Then ask if there is something you can do to make their jobs easier. Listen intently, write down what they tell you, and follow up quickly by fixing the problem.

You can adapt this key principle to any business of any size. A good example comes from Frank Richards, the president and CEO of a not-for-profit called America's Second Harvest of South Georgia. Frank, who credits Disney Institute training programs with helping him turn a nearly bankrupt company into a thriving organization, used to spend 80 percent of his time in his office and 20 percent on the floor of his sixty-thousand-square-foot facility. But after hearing about this concept at the Disney Institute, he flipped that ratio around. Now he spends 80 percent of his time in the warehouse and offices, visiting every department, chatting with employees, gathering information, and spotting problems before they become crises. He even improved on the idea of taking notes by installing at the end of every row of the warehouse a whiteboard, on which he writes down things that need attention—a food spill, a broken pallet, etc.—so that his managers are alerted to the problems without Frank's having to track them down. By the end of the day, virtually all the items he writes down have been taken care of, and Frank is far better informed than he was in the morning. I predict that someday soon Frank won't find much wrong on his rounds because he is teaching his team what to look for. At that point his daily walks will be shorter, and he'll have more time to grow his business. That is exactly what happens when you invest the time to get out and about.

I have to emphasize one thing: Get out and about *regularly*. If your people see you only once a week or a couple of times a month, they may change their behavior just because they know they are being observed. Plus they won't feel comfortable enough to tell you what you need to know. But when they see you often, they'll act the same way whether you are there or not. They'll know you really care and really listen, and will trust you enough to deliver the whole truth and nothing but.

2. Get a ground-level view. To the degree it's possible, observe your operations the way customers see them. When I was in charge of food and beverages at Marriott, I often showed up at one of the restaurants or bars looking like any other customer. When I became the general manager of a hotel, I actually lived in it for the first three months, and I learned things I would never have known otherwise. For example, I found out that at a certain hour in the morning it took about ten minutes for hot water to arrive on the fourteenth floor. At first the director of engineering did not believe me, but when I showed him my daily hot-water log and climbed up into the ceiling with him to investigate, we found that a closed valve in a recirculation line was slowing the release of the hot water. Who knows how many guests had opted to stay at a different hotel their next time in town because of that slow hot water?

When I worked at Disney World, I often threw on shorts and a baseball cap and took my grandkids to the park. We stood in lines, asked for directions, ate, drank, and bought merchandise. Believe me, it was very different from the view in a suit, and my observations led to several improvements. Waiting in the hot sun was a dose of reality that made me very supportive of spending money to add queues *inside* the attractions, where there was plenty of air conditioning. Because my grandchildren showed me the error of our ways, we started serving french fries with the hot dogs in kids' meals instead of cornmeal balls. (Since 2006 Disney has offered nutritionally balanced food for children, including more vegetables and fresh fruit side items.) I also learned that some rides were quite scary for kids of a certain age, so we started training Cast Members to explain the conditions to parents. My grandson Jullian was even responsible for a new policy at an Animal Kingdom attraction. You see, Jullian loved those carnival-type games where you win prizes by squirting water onto a target, but every time he played he got upset because an adult won. So he recommended that we have some rounds when only kids could play, no grown-ups allowed. Ever since we followed his suggestion, a lot of happy youngsters have walked away winners.

Whether your operation is the pit of a brokerage house, the call center of a Silicon Valley tech company, or the floor of a major retail outlet, you can find ways to experience it the way your customers do.

3. Meet regularly with direct reports. Don't just ask your direct reports if everything is OK and take yes for an answer. Everything is *never* OK. Hold substantive one-on-one meetings with them on a regular basis. When I met with my direct reports at Disney, I organized the conversations around what I called the Four Ps: people, processes, projects, and profit.

* **People:** Have them update you on *their* direct reports. Ask who the promising leaders are and how they're being developed for their next roles. Also find out who's *not* performing well and what's being done to get them on track.

* **Processes:** Have them explain what process changes they are working on to improve employee performance and customer experience.

* **Projects:** Have them describe the initiatives they're working on to upgrade the products and services they're responsible for.

✳ **Profit:** Have them give you status reports on their financial responsibilities, including sales figures, cost controls, and emerging problems.

Using this model with my direct reports kept me totally up-to-date on all the important issues. Once, Erin Wallace told me she had a gut feeling that one of her general managers was not as engaged in his operations as he should have been, but she wasn't sure how to handle it without hard evidence. I started paying closer attention to that manager's performance myself, and eventually the two of us were able to help him get on track. Today he's a very successful leader at Disney World.

As I mention in Chapter Three, I usually met with my direct reports in *their* offices, not mine. Try it. You can learn an awful lot by scanning the physical layout, watching people interact, and chatting with employees. It's worth the few extra minutes it takes to go to someone else's office. Maybe you can also use the exercise!

4. Assemble small groups. One of the most effective ways to gather information is to bring employees together to talk. I find that a group of ten or twelve people is the best size; it gives you a diversity of viewpoints while remaining intimate enough for everyone to feel relaxed and have enough time to speak. When I assembled such groups, I'd tell them, "I'm making decisions all week, and I know I don't know everything I need to know. That's why you're here today. I want to know what you're thinking, and if you don't feel comfortable telling me the whole truth in this room, go to Kinko's and send me an anonymous e-mail or a fax."

To encourage them to speak their minds, I phrased my questions in such a way that they knew I wanted to help them do their jobs better, not find fault with their performance. One of my favorite questions was: "What happens on your job that makes you want to quit?" Let's be honest, even in the best of jobs there's always something that makes people so frustrated that they think about walking out the door, and my question gave them permission to say so openly. An executive at Disney World (I'll call her Kate) once replied that she thought about quitting because she did not feel appreciated or trusted by people in another part of our organization. Having to justify every operating decision was wearing her out. So I talked with the manager who ran the other area and asked him to ratchet back the scrutiny and give Kate some breathing room to run her business. Things were not always 100 percent perfect after that, but they got considerably better, and Kate eventually moved up to a higher level in the company.

There are all kinds of ways to bring people together in small groups, whether for formal meetings, social events, or even a meal. Any setting is fine, as long as you create an atmosphere that encourages openness and honesty. You might want to have someone take notes on a laptop so you can focus all your attention on listening and still have an accurate record of what is said.

Small gatherings are especially important in times of change, like when you first take over a new position. I always devoted the first month on a job to fact-finding. I made checklists of things I needed to learn about every department, and I quickly got up to speed by meeting with managers in groups of about ten and asking questions like "What do you most want for your department right now?" In one hotel, for example, the banquet staff asked for more hangers for the coatroom; the restaurant team needed new silverware and wanted to serve more fresh fish; and housekeeping wanted to replace the carpet in the lobby. So I immediately sent someone out to buy hangers, ordered flatware, told the chef to add two fresh fish specials that very day, and had someone look into carpeting. Because the managers saw me respond quickly to *everyone's* request, they knew I didn't play favorites, and they kept on letting me know what they needed to get their jobs done.

5. Make them feel safe. When people come to you in confidence with a sensitive issue—a medical condition that hampers their performance, for example, or a complaint about a coworker—it's vital to make them feel comfortable and safe. As I suggest in Chapter Three, you might want to get out from behind your big desk and sit beside them. And give them your complete attention—no multitasking and no interruptions. If you want the truth, you have to put them at ease.

Keep in mind, however, that despite your best efforts, some people will always be afraid to speak up. Once I realized that, I made one of the best decisions of my career; I created a confidential e-mail address and a voice mail number so anyone at Disney World could communicate with me anonymously. I assured the Cast Members that the technology protected their anonymity; no one in the organization, including me, could identify the sender. If they revealed their names, I would get back to them, but if they did *not* feel safe doing so, I would still follow up on every issue they brought to my attention—from too-slow traffic lights to safety hazards that required immediate attention. As a result, the amount of candid information I received increased dramatically. I'm happy to say it is now common practice for Disney leaders to have confidential voice and e-mail systems.

Still, the best way to make people feel safe enough to speak the truth is to establish a trusting, comfortable relationship with each person. Once you do, be sure to preserve that trust by making people feel appreciated for coming forward. Always thank them for speaking their minds, whether or not their information was really useful. The positive reinforcement will encourage them to be honest in the future. Above all, don't shoot the messenger when you're told something upsetting. If you make someone regret telling you the truth, you're not likely to hear from him or her again. Remember the story of the goose that laid the golden eggs. Be nice to that goose; don't eat it for dinner or scare it to death.

6. Probe for the whole story. Let's face it, people won't always tell you everything you need to know. It's not so much that they lie as that they leave out significant details, either because they're afraid to deliver unpleasant news or because the truth might make them look bad. To some extent, it comes with the territory; leaders are kept in the dark, just like parents. If you doubt this, think back to when you were a teenager. Did you tell your parents everything? Well, neither do your kids or your employees—unless they trust you 100 percent.

I worked very hard to earn that trust at Disney World, and even then I didn't always get the whole story. Cast Members often came to me in confidence and told me they were not happy with their jobs or the way they were being treated. But that was just the headline. I learned to probe deeper. I'd ask questions like "Is there anything else you want to tell me?" and on many occasions they would fidget a bit and say, "Well, yes." Then the whole story would start to emerge.

Probing for the deeper truth is especially important with high-priority issues, like safety. At Marriott the standard accident reports seldom revealed the whole story, so I changed the policy in the hotel I ran: In addition to filling out a report, any associate who had an accident had to come see me, with his or her manager, and explain exactly what happened. I interrogated those employees the way Judge Judy or any tough judge would so I could make sure it never happened again. More often than not I unearthed the real cause of the accident, and we were able to adjust the operating guidelines and training procedures to prevent a recurrence. I instituted a similar process at Disney World, reviewing new accidents every morning and following up with the appropriate management team. Over the next eighteen months we reduced our accident frequency by over 50 percent.

If you want to know the *rest* of the story, pay close attention to what's being said and what's not being said when talking to your employees. Look for subtle clues to what the person is really thinking, like body language, facial expressions, or changes in behavior. Take careful notes, ask detailed clarifying questions, and keep digging deeper—in a nonthreatening manner—until you get to the truth. Once you do, shift the focus to the future. A good question to conclude with is: "What would you like me to do?" This underscores your seriousness and can lead to practical improvements. Whatever the person's response, make sure you're clear about what steps, if any, you're going to take next, and always follow through.

7. Answer the tough questions. Remember, a leader's job is not just to *ask* questions but to *answer* them as well. If you really want honesty, you'd better demonstrate that you're willing to answer hard questions. Early in my career, when I was running a busy restaurant, I was once humiliated in a meeting because I couldn't answer some of the staff's questions. Ever since then I've made it a point to do what smart public figures do before press conferences: anticipate the toughest questions, prepare the answers, and mentally rehearse them. I also learned some things that many public figures have not:

* Avoid using formulas and clichés; they make you sound insincere even if you're not.

* Don't pretend to know something you don't; in my experience, the answer that builds the most trust is: "I don't know, but I'll get back to you on that."

* Always tell the truth, even if it means admitting a mistake; as we learned from Watergate and other scandals, actions are usually forgiven, but cover-ups are not.

In 2004, at a leadership conference hosted by Disney University, I conducted three sessions called "The Top Ten Questions You Wish People Would Not Ask You." From the thousand or so Disney leaders who attended, I garnered the twenty toughest questions they're asked. Then I answered them, both at the conference and in *The Main Street Diary*, so everyone in the company could learn from the exchange. The important thing was not my answers as such, but preparing future leaders for the questions they will be called upon to answer someday. Since then leaders in all kinds of organizations whom I've coached or taught at the Disney Institute have adapted those same questions to their own circumstances so they could be prepared with answers. Below are a few examples. How would you answer them? What are the toughest questions for *your* organization?

* Why don't people in my position get paid more?

* Things aren't like they used to be. Why did they change, and how can we restore the good things we've lost?

* How do you work with someone you don't like or trust?

* How can we honor our seniority-based scheduling system and also consider the individual needs of our employees?

* How can we retain quality employees in the face of our need to reduce expenditures for health care and other benefits?

* Why does my health care plan keep getting more expensive while I have fewer benefits?

* Why does our CEO earn millions per year and I can't get a modest raise?

* Isn't this latest initiative to streamline procedures really just an excuse to reduce head count?

* Will the company maintain its pension or 401(k) program in the future?

* What is the greatest obstacle to workplace diversity?

* How we can increase the level of trust for us as leaders, and how can we increase trust within our own leadership team?

* As a young employee who cares about the future, how can I develop career traction within the company?

* How should we respond to direct reports asking how they can get to the next level when we're not sure they're ready for it?

* What is the best way to focus on flawless performance while still allowing people room to learn from their mistakes and grow?

* What is the best way to handle the politics of a large organization?

* How can we motivate people to be fully committed and to make the extra effort to achieve our goals?

8. Get formal feedback about yourself. Perhaps the hardest information for leaders to gather is honest opinions about their own strengths and weaknesses. That's why it's so important to institute regular feedback mechanisms for every leader in your organization, especially yourself. Because this feedback should come from more than one source, get anonymous evaluations from your supervisor, your peers, and your direct reports.

I can tell you from personal experience that it's extremely eye-opening to see yourself as others see you. One year my own results in Disney's Cast excellence survey, which I describe in Chapter Five, indicated that I played favorites. Stunned to discover that my direct reports thought that way, I gathered them together and said, "You're sending me a message here. Let's talk about it." The first person to speak up said, "You don't ask for my opinion, Lee. It seems that you only value what Erin and Karl have to say and that I'm not important." If feedback like that had come from just one person, I might have believed it was his imagination. But three others thought the same way. "You're probably right," I said. "Shame on me. I'm going to work on it." I did work on it, and as a result, the dynamics of the team improved dramatically.

Again, getting feedback is great, but it amounts to very little if you don't do anything with the information. Had I dismissed their concerns, defended my behavior, or pretended to care and done nothing about it, I would have lost their respect, and I'd have been forced to operate in a truth vacuum because they would never have opened up to me again.

Frank Richards, the nonprofit CEO we met earlier, took this advice to heart after hearing it at a Disney Institute seminar. Upon returning to his organization in rural Georgia, he pulled his entire staff together for a series of brainstorming sessions on how to gather the most useful feedback. This led to a system of annual surveys, and now once a year every leader in the organization is rated anonymously on how he or she treats, manages, and cares for his or her employees. One year Frank learned something important about himself: His direct reports said he didn't look at them when they spoke to him. It seems he's always been a good multitasker, and he feels most productive when he's doing more than one thing at a time. But when he saw that it bothered his direct reports, he realized it wasn't always appropriate. "When someone meets with me now," he says, "I put everything away, turn off the computer, and give them my full attention." Those annual surveys have been a huge factor in the company's turnaround.

9. Constantly evaluate your spending. One final point: Knowing what's going on in your organization also means keeping track of how your money is being spent. Constantly reviewing your invoices to keep track of your spending is one of your most important jobs as a leader.

When I first became a hotel manager, I made it a policy to approve all invoices myself instead of allowing department managers to do so. This way I could see firsthand what we were paying for various goods and services. At one point, for instance, I noticed that we'd started to pay a lot more for tomatoes. It turned out that McDonald's had started putting tomatoes on its burgers, dramatically altering the supply-and-demand ratio nationwide and driving up the prices. So I told the chef to eliminate tomatoes from our salads. He did not think it was a good idea at first, but he quickly found ways to make great-tasting salads without tomatoes. We saved a ton of money, and not one guest complained (nowadays most restaurants do not have tomatoes in their salads—not *good* tomatoes at any rate). While I might have read in a newspaper that McDonald's had added tomatoes to its burgers, I would not have appreciated the impact on my business if I hadn't been reviewing the invoices.

Another time I saw expensive items I didn't recognize on invoices from the maintenance department. When I asked to see these items, the maintenance supervisor could not produce them. It turned out that some employees had taken them home to resell. We might never have uncovered this internal theft if I had not been personally keeping track of invoices.

More often than not a careful review of your company finances will uncover unnecessary or excessive expenditures somewhere in the organization. When this happens, it's up to you to figure out ways to cut back—the way I did with the tomatoes. But you don't have to do it alone. If you hire and train great people, they'll help you meet these challenges. In the difficult days following 9/11, when the executives and managers at Walt Disney World were desperately looking for ways to cut costs, we called upon frontline Cast Members for ideas. Their response was extraordinary. Some of them came up with a process to make the bus routes more efficient, thereby saving on gas and cutting down on labor costs. Others suggested landscaping changes: mowing the grass less often or planting flowers only in the visible places where the Guests could enjoy them. Bartenders recommended sanitizing and reusing the plastic stir sticks instead of throwing them away and cutting lemons in six pieces instead of four. The ideas saved a few hundred dollars here and a few thousand there, adding up to enough reductions to keep us going at full speed without laying off one person.

Such is the power of asking motivated people to think of ways to cut costs. But you don't have to wait for a crisis. At Disney we implemented a policy that called upon managers and their teams to find ways to knock one to three percent off their budgets every year. The only rule was that nothing they did could adversely affect the Guest experience. Prior to this, cost-saving ideas came up almost haphazardly—and infrequently. But once we required managers to look actively for ways to cut costs, they did so consistently, with no loss in Guest satisfaction, and the savings were tremendous. Think of it this way: I'm sure you and your family are eager to find ways to eliminate unnecessary expenditures, yet coming up with ideas is probably a matter of chance—maybe you stumble upon a going-out-of-business sale or happen to get a promotional rate on a rental car—but what if you kept careful track of all your expenses and made an agreement to cut twenty-five dollars a week from your budget? I bet you'd find a lot more places to save—without even noticing a difference in your quality of life.

Point is, there is gold in your invoices. After all, they are the most reliable record of your spending practices. If you take the time to review them, you'll be far more informed about where your company's hard-earned money is going, and you'll be in a much better position to generate ideas for cutting costs without jeopardizing productivity or quality.

No matter what business you're in, your decisions are only as good as the information they're based on. As a leader you need to know your operation as well as you know your own home, and you need to know your employees as well as you know your own children. Don't ever get caught saying, "I wish I'd known."

ACTION STEPS

* Walk through employee and customer areas several times a day, especially at the beginning of the day.

* Be visible in the workplace to employees and customers.

* Experience your operation from the customers' and employees' points of view regularly.

* Find ways to create comfortable relationships with everyone in your workplace.

* Make yourself accessible by being available 24/7 and by getting out and about.

* Meet with your direct reports regularly, and discuss the Four Ps.

* Hold forums often so your employees can tell you what's really going on.

* Learn to read between the lines of what people tell you.

* Follow through on every idea and concern your employees share with you. Always keep your word.

* Demonstrate care, consideration, respect, sensitivity, and confidentiality.

* Ask your manager and frontline employees what results they are measuring.

* Dig deeper, and deeper still, until you learn the whole truth.

CHAPTER NINE

STRATEGY #7

BURN THE FREE FUEL

W hen I was the director of food and beverages at the Chicago Marriott, the banquet manager who worked for me was a steadfast commander named Eddie Towfighnia. At the time it was not uncommon for the hotel to be simultaneously serving banquets of two thousand people on one floor and five thousand on another, and Eddie made every function run smoothly and on time. He had a remarkable knack for keeping as many as four hundred servers organized, efficient, and on their toes, handling every detail with such ease you'd think he was hosting a cocktail party in his home. One night, as the guests for two huge banquets poured into the hotel, it dawned on me just how indispensable Eddie was. "Without him, I'm dead," I thought.

The next morning, I wrote Eddie a letter praising his talent and telling him how much I depended on him. I underscored the message by adding, "If you ever think of leaving, please come and talk with me before making the final decision."

A few months later my wife, Priscilla, and I were invited to dinner with Eddie and his wife, Joyce. When we entered their home, I was stunned to see the letter I'd sent him, handsomely framed and hanging in a prominent place in the foyer. At first I was somewhat embarrassed. Then I realized how important that letter must have been to him and how proud it must have made him feel. I was deeply moved.

From that day forward I made it a high priority to express my appreciation for the people who worked for me. Writing that letter to Eddie took about five minutes. Did it make him better at his job? Maybe not, but only because he was so skilled already. But I believe strongly that it made him a better leader. Why? Because knowing how great that letter made him feel, he was far more likely to express his appreciation for the chefs, servers, and others who made his banquet rooms hum, and that, in turn, made *them* better leaders.

Appreciation, recognition, encouragement: ARE. Together they make up a cost-free, fully sustainable fuel, one that builds self-confidence and self-esteem, boosts individual and team performance, and keeps an organization running cleanly and smoothly. ARE is more powerful than the fuels that make engines roar and space shuttles soar, because it propels human energy and motivation. And unlike costly, nonrenewable fuels like oil and gas, its supply is inexhaustible. You can give out ARE all day long, at home and at work, and wake up the next morning with a full tank. In fact, the more we use, the more there is, because every time people receive some ARE they discover more of their own internal supply and start giving away the overflow.

Here's another difference between ARE and fossil fuel: Instead of using too much of it, we don't use enough. If leaders were as extravagant with ARE as the rest of us are with oil, the world would be a better place. If you think I'm exaggerating, ask yourself how many times you've thought, "I'm getting way too much appreciation, recognition, and encouragement! I can't take any more." I know I never had such thoughts. When I ask people at my seminars if they feel overappreciated for their hard work and good results, I never fail to get a roomful of nervous laughs and head shakes.

Like most managers, I didn't fully realize the importance of ARE until later in my career. It took a powerful experience to teach me the lesson. In 1973, about three weeks into my new job as director of restaurants at the Philadelphia Marriott, I was struggling with some very difficult issues. Some of my direct reports were not performing very well, and one of them thought *I* should be reporting to *him*. Plus some ill-conceived marketing programs were putting a heavy strain on the room service department. Making a tough situation even harder, I was getting no feedback on my performance. I hadn't seen or heard from either my boss or the general manager, not even once. Feeling terribly overwhelmed and insecure, I told Priscilla, "I think taking this job was the biggest mistake of my life." The very next day I received a note from the general manager. It read:

Dear Lee:

I am sorry that I have not seen you since you started. I have been tied up in Washington working on some new projects. I just want to tell you that I am hearing great things from everyone about what a great job you are doing. We are really happy to have you on our team. You are making a difference.

Sincerely,

Richard

I know that's an exact quote because I still have the letter. That's how much it meant to me. It was a turbo boost to my self-confidence just when I needed it most. In fact, *everyone* needs ARE—and not just when times are hard. Anyone who says he or she doesn't need it probably just wants to be recognized as humble. I don't mind telling you that no matter how successful I became, I never stopped feeling great whenever I was appreciated, recognized, or encouraged by a leader. Even when I was a top executive at one of the world's most famous companies, I was energized by a note from Al Weiss, my boss at *Walt Disney World®* Resort, which read: "Lee, you are a great partner. You do a great job, and I hope you stay with me for another 15 years." That note made my day. I took it home and showed it to my wife and mother-in-law, and the next day I told Al how much I appreciated it. That's what I mean by inexhaustible fuel; getting that ARE from Al made me want to give some right back to him.

Unfortunately, even though we all need ARE, we don't give enough of it to the people who work for us. It's not that we don't know how; most of us know it instinctively. When a child puts a square block in the square hole, for instance, we always say, "Good job." When a child tries to put a square block in a round hole and fails, we say, "Good job, try again." We know exactly why it's important to bolster a child's confidence and self-esteem, but we often forget that grown-ups need encouragement too. In fact, in many businesses, when that block goes into the wrong hole, instead of saying, "Good try, give it another shot," leaders belittle people or threaten them with termination.

Never underestimate the emotional impact you have as a leader. Over the years she worked for me, I sent my administrative assistant, Marsha Davis, special thank-you notes on several occasions. One day, I discovered that she kept them under glass on her desk for everyone to see. That was how much my appreciation meant to her, and not even Shakespeare could capture in a thank-you note what Marsha gave back in loyalty and commitment. In fact, as I walked around Disney World and visited people in their offices, I would occasionally see a thank-you note I had once sent pinned to a Cast Member's wall. One memorable night, when I was having dinner at the Wilderness Lodge, the server took one of those notes out of his wallet to show it to me; I had sent it to him five years earlier. And I assure you I was hardly the only leader at Disney World whose thank-you notes were cherished. It's pretty common because ARE is an integral part of the company culture. You can make it an integral part of yours as well, regardless of the industry you're in or even the country you're in.

If you don't appreciate, respect, and encourage those you lead, they'll give you only halfhearted effort or, worse, sabotage you or leave you high and dry. Great leaders know that, and they look for opportunities to give out the free fuel of ARE in an authentic, specific, and timely manner. The following tips will help you find those opportunities and follow through on them.

1. Spend meaningful time with employees. You'd be surprised how much it means to people when their leader chooses to be with them—not looking over their shoulders but helping them, getting to know them, asking what they think and feel, and simply enjoying their company. Employees know how valuable your time is, so if you spend some of it with them, they figure they must be pretty valuable too.

As I mention in Chapter Eight, when I was at Disney World, I spent about half my time out and about, visiting with Cast

Members. I asked them to walk me through their operations and show me all the good things they were doing for Guests. They proudly talked about new Take 5s they had performed, or gave me a taste of a new dish they'd added to the menu, or took me for a ride on a newly renovated attraction. Those walks took up a lot of precious time, but they were worth every minute, because they not only made me better informed but gave me an opportunity to dole out ARE. The message I was sending was simple but profound: "You matter, and I know it. We couldn't do it without you."

Another great way to spend meaningful time with employees is to participate in employee events. Many departments at Disney World hold small gatherings to give out performance awards or to celebrate someone's retirement, the birth of a child, or a promotion. I was invited to many of these and to all the larger events, and I did my utmost to attend. I scheduled them in my trusty Day-Timer and showed up whenever possible. By dropping by for even a few minutes, I showed the Cast Members how much I appreciated them.

It always surprises me that many leaders don't bother to show up at such events. Apparently, they consider it a waste of time. I tell them that strong leaders have to do the little things that go a very long way. Why do you think politicians hug babies and eat bad food at county fairs? In the business world, you're not looking for votes, but you do want the equivalent: commitment. To get that commitment, you need to let your employees know that *you* are committed to *them*. Showing up says that they matter to you, and if that inspires even one person to do a better job, isn't it worth the time?

That goes for outside events as well as official company festivities. Don't think it's beneath you to appear at a birthday party for someone you barely know or to attend an employees' bowling night. I must admit that I didn't always want to go out in the evening after a hard day at work or to show up for a Saturday afternoon party when I could have been with my family. But unless I had a serious scheduling conflict, I did my best to be at every event I was invited to, and often Priscilla would go with me. Over the years I attended many a late-night party and many a breakfast party for our third-shift Cast Members, who worked from 10:00 P.M. to 6:00 A.M. The truth is, I was almost always glad I went because being around the Cast was a positive experience. And the Cast always appreciated that I—or we, if Priscilla was with me—chose to spend time with them.

Bottom line: When you're a leader, you're well served by being visible. I always found that seeing employees with their hair down and meeting their children and spouses added a personal touch to my relationships with them that made working together easier and more pleasant. And you give out tremendous amounts of ARE just by showing up.

2. Recognize employees by name. When I made my daily rounds at Walt Disney World, I did my best to call everyone by name. Since I had so many names to remember, I started recording them in my BlackBerry, along with the names of their family members and other unique things about them, like the classes they were taking or their plans for the future, so I could refresh my memory before I saw them. If you think it's not important to remember names, think back to when you were young and an authority figure called you by yours. I was reminded of this just recently, when I was driving my twelve-year-old grandson Jullian home after football practice. He's new to the sport and not as big as most of his teammates because he's younger, having skipped a grade. As a result, he doesn't get to play as much as he wants to, even in practice. As he clambered into the car that day, he looked despondent. "Papi, I didn't get to play at all today," he said. I reminded him that he was younger and smaller than the others, but that didn't help much. He said he didn't like football after all and might not play next year.

The next afternoon, I picked up a very different Jullian. He was beaming when he got into the car, once again in love with football. He said he'd gotten into the action several times that day and had performed well. Then he added, with great pride, "The coach knows my name." He had been given a big dose of recognition.

You'll see the same difference in your employees when you recognize them as individuals. So don't underestimate the emotional impact of calling someone by name. Believe me, if you say "Hi, Hank" and shake his hand, Hank will feel a whole lot different than if you just wave to him as you pass by.

3. Catch them doing something right. As I've mentioned, one quality leaders must have is an astute ability to evaluate employees and give them quality feedback. Unfortunately, too many managers are terrific at singling out shortcomings or areas that need improvement but not so good at acknowledging behavior that ought to be encouraged. Like good parents, the best leaders accentuate the positive and reinforce it constantly. They know that people do their best work when they're confident, and nothing fuels self-confidence like positive feedback from a leader. You have to go through the heart to get to the brain, and ARE goes straight to the heart. And it feels so good that the brain thinks, "I'll do that again next time."

So train yourself to notice the right stuff, not just the wrong. And when you see it, reinforce it quickly—*immediately,* if possible—because the smaller the gap between the behavior and the appreciation, the stronger the message. And make the feedback specific; let people know exactly what they're doing right. A generic "Thank you for your help" is not as powerful as "You did a great job organizing that meeting on Friday, and I really appreciate the effort that went into it." Also, deliver the reinforcement in a form that's appropriate for the circumstances and the individual. In some cases a tangible reward, whether it's a monetary bonus or a lapel pin, might be appropriate, while in other cases a personal e-mail or a handwritten note might be best. Some people thrive on hoopla, while others are averse to the spotlight. Take this into account. If you sense someone is reserved or shy, don't show that person your appreciation by announcing it on the loudspeaker or throwing him or her a party. There are quieter ways to acknowledge such employees.

I always made it a high priority to recognize the contributions of Cast Members in as many ways as I could think of. Every morning, when I got to my office in Orlando, I read through all the letters we'd received from Guests, and whenever one of them singled out a Cast Member for exceptional service, I made a copy, wrote a note of thanks in the corner, attached an award pin, and sent it on to the person's manager. Why not send it directly to the Cast Member? Because sending it to the manager meant that the individual would get a double dip of recognition and maybe even a triple dip if he or she were acknowledged in front of peers. I estimate that I sent out about seven hundred notes and award pins a month to the frontline Cast.

About those award pins: I introduced a few different types. Two had Mickey Mouse figures on them, one with the words "You Created Magic" and the other with "You're a Disney Star." A simple pin, given for leadership excellence, had only the word "leadership" against the familiar logo of a mouse face and ears. When someone displayed really outstanding leadership, by heading a successful project, for instance, or implementing a difficult change in a work process, I sent a thank-you note on a personalized card and stuck a leadership pin on it. Another pin, sporting a picture of the Seven Dwarfs in a cheerleader-style pyramid, recognizes excellence in following the 7 Guest Service Guidelines, which I describe in Chapter Six. Then there's a pin that's given to Cast Members whose contributions are recognized in *The Main Street Diary*. It says, "Congratulations! You made a difference by being a source of joy and inspiration."

The pins cost a buck or two each, but if pride has a price, they're worth millions. They not only encouraged Cast Members to repeat the kind of performance that earned them the pin but also served as visual reminders to others of exactly what the company means by excellence. Even though no one is supposed to wear one on his or her costume, I often ran into Cast Members who pinned them on anyway.

Disney has other unique ways to dole out ARE. The Recognize Everyday Magic tool kit, for example, makes it easy for leaders to acknowledge Cast Members as they go about their business every day. These kits consist of Recognition Sticky Notes, Recognition Thank You Cards and Envelopes, Recognition Praise Cards, and other items to give to people who do something special, particularly in the area of safety. As a means of instilling pride in performance these inexpensive items are as valuable as gold.

What can your organization give that would have a similar emotional impact? A gesture that may seem silly to you might mean the world to an employee, and it will be repaid in loyalty, dedication, and extra effort. For many workers, just hearing their leader say thank you on the phone or even on a voice mail would make their day.

I know what you're thinking: This is great, but what if you catch them doing something *wrong*? Well, constructive criticism can also be a form of ARE—if you give it in the right way at the right time. When you correct people properly, you're saying, in effect, "I think enough of you to tell you how to realize more of your potential by doing your job even better." It shows that you respect them and you want them to be successful. Just remember to be thoughtful, tactful, and upbeat with your feedback. And it bears repeating: Never criticize someone in front of others.

4. Make it public. Most organizations know it's important to formally recognize employees. That's why annual celebrations, award ceremonies, and company picnics are so common. Disney is no exception in that regard. In addition to giving out individual awards at various occasions, the company honors *all* Cast Members with its annual Cast Holiday Celebration. This isn't just a one-night event. From late November to early December, Cast Members and their families and Guests can visit any of the theme parks for free and even receive family photos, holiday gifts, and special discounts on meals and merchandise. In addition, every department has a budget for annual parties, which are often held during the summer at Little Lake Bryan, a recreational park a few miles away. The park, with facilities for swimming, boating, and other sports, is open year-round for the exclusive use of Disney Cast Members and their families.

But why restrict appreciation to periodic occasions that might come to feel commonplace? Deserving employees should be recognized in front of their peers whenever it's appropriate. This not only enhances positive reinforcement but also motivates other employees to emulate the behavior that's being rewarded. It serves another function as well: It enables managers throughout the organization to learn about talented employees who might otherwise go undiscovered. At Walt Disney World, bestowing appreciation is considered so important that the company even has a position called manager of Cast recognition.

There are countless ways to spotlight exceptional contributions. Each year, for instance, Disney World recognizes as many as nine hundred top performers by giving them a once-in-a-lifetime Partner in Excellence Award for career achievement in one of three categories: Guest satisfaction, Cast excellence, or operational/financial. The recipients and their Guests are honored at a fancy awards dinner, with excellent food and such distinguished speakers as Colin Powell. Along with a special partners pin, each honoree is given a bronze statue of Walt Disney and Mickey Mouse. Why Walt and Mickey? Because those two were the company's first partners in excellence.

Awards dinners are certainly a great way to publicly recognize your employees, but public ARE should be an ongoing feature of organizational life. That's where Disney World, and the thousands of people from other companies who implement what they learn at Disney Institute training programs, really stand out. For instance, I mentioned that every issue of *The Main Street Diary* contains eight or ten letters from Guests describing the memorable service they received from particular Cast Members. But it doesn't stop there. Disney managers are encouraged to read those Guest letters to their entire teams during their pre-shift meetings and to present the award pins in front of the recipients' peers. Other Guest letters are printed in *Eyes & Ears*, the biweekly company-wide newsletter. I only wish I could have reproduced *all* the letters of praise, but that would have been impossible, since we received hundreds of them a week.

I must highlight another terrific Disney ARE feature, Great Service Fanatic cards. Any day, at any time, leaders and peers can fill out one of these folded cards and give it to a Cast Member who did something to surprise or delight the Guests. The recipient keeps a duplicate of the card, which describes his or her special performance in detail, and gives the original to his or her leader to sign. Each month a number of cards are randomly drawn, and a "Prize Patrol" goes around making award presentations to the winning Fanatics, complete with prizes, balloons, pixie dust, and photo ops. You can't imagine how much this little celebration means to the recipients and how strongly it reinforces the qualities of performance excellence that Disney stands for.

Finally, here's a surprisingly effective way to give out ARE publicly: Do it *privately*. Am I contradicting myself? No. What I mean is this: You can express appreciation for someone when he or she is not even present by simply telling other people what a great job the person is doing or by describing something special that he or she did. I discovered this method at Disney World one day when Erin Wallace told me, "I hear you're saying good things about me behind my back." The comment really caught my attention. From then on I always remembered to speak well of people in their absence. It's a powerful means of positive reinforcement precisely because it's not likely to stay private; nine times out of ten, the person you praise will hear about it, and so will others, who will want you to speak well of them too.

5. Include their families. Whenever you can arrange for an employee's spouse, children, friends, partner, or other loved ones to share in the recognition, do it. And any time you have an opportunity to express appreciation for an employee's loved ones themselves, take advantage of it. A strong support system at home is a silent contributor to good performance, and loved ones often pay a hefty price for an employee's dedication. They too deserve some ARE. At Disney, family members are often invited to presentations where Cast Members are being recognized. Recently, for example, the company had a little surprise party for Frank Yiannas, the director of safety and health, to celebrate a national award he'd received. His wife, brother, and father were present, and the pride on their faces showed enough ARE to fuel years of quality performance by everyone present. As Frank said, "Having my family there made it extra special." I know the feeling; at my retirement party, Disney executives made sure to invite my closest friends and my entire family. And because my three grandchildren, Tristan, Margot, and Jullian, were in France and couldn't attend, my colleagues made a video of them congratulating their papi and showed it at the party. That made a special occasion *really* special.

But as I've said, why stop at special occasions? Why not send occasional thank-you notes to the spouses and significant others of your loyal employees? After all, they're invested in your company too, even though they don't work there. It's a small investment of time, but it can be a powerful booster shot to your employees' commitment. And don't forget their kids. You don't have to run a theme park to do something special for the children of your employees. Here's a story I heard recently, from my son, Daniel, who works at Disney World. A Cast Member named Andy Nanasi had just completed an extensive project he had been working on for a month. It had entailed many late nights and long hours, and when it was done, he said, he and his leader, Robin Zais, were "jazzed about what we had accomplished." Three days later Andy's daughters, ages seven and nine, came to him with big, proud smiles on their faces. They said they had received a letter from "Miss Robin" in the mail and wanted to read it to him. The letter said, "Your daddy did an awesome job on a project and has worked really hard. I would like you both to take these gift certificates to Cold Stone Creamery and take him out for ice cream to celebrate."

"It was an incredibly emotional moment and one that filled me with pride," said Andy. "This by far is the most memorable and best recognition any leader has ever provided." It was indeed a brilliant form of ARE, and it would not have been possible if Robin hadn't taken the time to get to know Andy and his family over the four years they'd worked together.

6. Recognize and encourage good ideas. I've mentioned several times that creating a culture of participation leads to an abundance of useful ideas from all levels of an organization. Recognizing those ideas and showing that you're following up on them are in themselves an important form of ARE. At Disney World, where harvesting Cast Member ideas is a way of life, each department is encouraged to find its own way of recognizing those contributions. Phil Holmes, vice president of the Magic Kingdom theme park, for example, created an eight-page, full-color quarterly newsletter titled *You Said . . . We Listened . . .* that consists almost entirely of Cast Members' suggestions ("You Said") followed by the leadership response to each one ("We Listened"). One recent edition had about sixty ideas—for example: "You Said . . . Engineering needs to reduce the amount of paper required for Attractions Maintenance. We Listened . . . and implemented new handheld data tracking devices which have reduced paperwork dramatically" and "You Said . . . Guests have difficulty reading the menu boards at Pecos Bill Café. We Listened . . . and moved the menu boards forward, plus added additional lighting to them."

Is there any reason you couldn't produce something similar in your organization? If you want the support of your employees, you need to recognize their contributions, no matter how small or ordinary they might seem. And nothing says appreciation like following through on their suggestions and requests.

7. Give extra ARE to frontline employees. I strongly suggest paying particular attention to frontline employees. They often get overlooked when leaders dole out positive recognition, and they are often the most likely to be degraded, reprimanded, and given heat from customers. From my first day as a manager, I vowed to treat people in frontline hourly positions with extra dignity. I knew firsthand how demanding those jobs could be because I'd held many myself. As a farm boy with no college degree I waited tables, made beds, and worked in kitchens for several years before my career took off, and I knew the many subtle ways that frontline workers can be humiliated by leaders. I also knew that humiliated employees are not committed ones. Maybe they give only 50 percent of their effort instead of 100 percent; worse, they try to get revenge by gossiping, quitting abruptly, suing the company, or even stealing.

At Disney everyone at every level is made to feel that he or she is an essential part of the organization, whether sweeping sidewalks, busing tables, or selling souvenirs. "You *are* Disney," I told people on my rounds, and they believed it because I believed it. I also made sure that other leaders delivered the same message. Those who followed through on that advice experienced far less turnover and absenteeism and enjoyed a whole lot more commitment and loyalty. And this paid off in measurable business success.

So make sure to treat frontline employees as respectfully as you treat those in higher positions, if not more so, even when you have to discipline or fire them. You can be tough, and you can tell it like it is, but your frontline employees should always know that you're on their side and that you appreciate what they bring to your organization.

8. Make ARE a natural part of your routine. As I said earlier, great leaders are environmentalists. If you want to attract and keep the best employees, you have to create a wonderful environment for them, and I assure you, recognition, appreciation, and encouragement are as important to a healthy workplace as clean air and water are to a healthy planet. So don't be stingy. There is no excuse for not giving away copious amounts of ARE. I've heard all the excuses, believe me, and none of them makes sense. Some leaders say they are just not comfortable expressing appreciation face-to-face; it is an emotional act, and it makes them uneasy. If that's the case, use notes, pins, certificates, publications, and other methods that don't involve speaking to the person directly. On the basis of my experience, there's a very good chance that eventually, when you see the results of ARE, you'll want the pleasure of delivering it in person.

Other managers are afraid that employees will become self-satisfied and slack off if they get too much praise. Nonsense. In this day and age the carrot is a much better motivator than the stick. As I say in my speeches to executives, if you think the Pyramids wouldn't have been built if the Egyptians hadn't whipped their slaves into shape, think again. Maybe they would have gone up even faster, with lower costs and fewer runaways, if they'd treated the workers better. Another excuse I've heard in recent years is this: "What if I say a person is doing well and then his performance declines and I have to let him go? The recognition could be used against me in a court of law." Again, nonsense. If you offer only negative feedback, your employees can use *that* against you just as easily, or they'll simply quit because they feel unappreciated. The best way to prevent a performance decline in the first place is to give away lots of ARE. That's how to make a good employee even better.

Remember, while pins, prizes, and special celebrations are terrific, ordinary, everyday ARE is just as powerful—and in many ways *more* so. Just keep in mind the Four Expectations of All Employees as you interact with your people.

* Make them feel special.

* Treat them as individuals.

* Respect them.

* Make them knowledgeable.

If you can make this a natural part of your behavior, you will turn the workaday world into someplace special, and you will be recognized as an inspirational leader who cares. To help you remember to do this, you might even schedule it into your planner or whatever method you use to track your to-do list. Every day I used to write down in my Day-Timer the names of deserving people I wanted to acknowledge, not just employees who performed well or did something exceptional but those who needed extra support, whether they were injured, had lost loved ones, or had children who were struggling in school. Remember, for some, a workplace with heart can be a place of refuge.

9. Watch your language. Words matter. So make sure your workplace vocabulary conveys the appreciation and respect you have for your employees. I recently participated in a leadership seminar with Frances Hesselbein, the former CEO of the Girl Scouts of the U.S.A., current chairman of the Leader to Leader Institute, and author of an excellent book titled *Hesselbein on Leadership*. Frances, who is recognized as one of the world's most effective leaders, made me smile when she said, "When is the last time you heard someone say, 'I can't wait to be a subordinate'?" In her view, terms like "subordinate"—which have implications such as "underling," "inferior," and "lower"—are becoming obsolete and ought to be replaced by words like "associate," "partner," and "team member."

Don't underestimate the power of word choices. Language evolves slowly, and it's sometimes hard to replace familiar words without sounding silly. But if you can find substitutes for unflattering terms and come up with language that captures the spirit of your organization the way Disney did with "Cast" and "onstage," your employees will feel more respected, appreciated, and valued.

Bill Marriott taught me a lot about the power of ARE when I resigned from his company to join Disney. He personally called me and told me how much the company valued me. He said that he did not want to see me leave, but since I *was* leaving, he wanted to wish me well. I never forgot his kindness and thoughtfulness. Here was a man who was running a multibillion-dollar company, and he took the time to pick up the phone and wish me well. This is just one of the reasons he is considered one of America's great business leaders.

Because I learned from people like Bill, I estimate that I personally fueled seven to eight thousand Disney Cast Members a year with ARE, and it paid off big-time because each of them was motivated to work at a higher level. Remember, it's contagious. Each person who receives ARE from you will have more of it to give to his or her coworkers, colleagues, and customers. It's not only free fuel but the main ingredient for creating a culture of magic.

ACTION STEPS

✳ Spend meaningful time with your employees and direct reports.

✳ Participate in and be visible at employee events.

✳ Make a point of remembering names and saying thank you.

✳ Model great performance actively and visibly.

✳ Greet everyone you come into contact with.

✳ Be conscious of the impact of your presence and your interactions with people.

✳ Find ways to celebrate the personal achievements and victories of your employees, and don't forget to include their families, friends, and loved ones.

✳ Carry some special recognition pins in your pocket to give out.

✳ Make a point of letting people know specifically what they're doing right.

✳ Always notice performance, positive or negative, and provide feedback promptly.

* Coach and train employees on the spot in better ways to perform their jobs.

* Don't tolerate poor performance or ignore performance issues.

* Publicly and privately recognize improvement or great performance.

* Train your teams to know what great performance looks like.

* Use your day planner to remind you to dispense ARE all day, every day.

* Create an inspiring vocabulary that makes people feel respected.

CHAPTER TEN

STRATEGY #8

STAY AHEAD OF THE PACK

The written version of the Disney Great Leader Strategies begins with this statement: "In times of drastic change, it is the learners who inherit the future. The learned usually find themselves equipped to live in a world that no longer exists." In other words, great leaders need to be lifelong learners.

In today's ever-changing world, keeping up with the times is absolutely critical. No matter what business or industry you're in, if you don't stay current with what's going on—from social and cultural developments to technological breakthroughs to world news—your competition will zoom ahead of you, your customers will abandon you, and you won't be able to meet the responsibilities of leadership.

In the hospitality industry, for instance, hotels that don't meet the needs of the digital age by providing wireless Internet access in every room will find themselves quickly losing a lot of customers and missing out on a good deal of revenue. And restaurants that don't respond quickly to America's growing concern about health and nutrition by offering low-fat dishes, allergy-safe ingredients, or nonsmoking areas will quickly fall behind the pack as well. One reason that the restaurants at *Walt Disney World®* Resort maintain a worldwide reputation for quality is that the chefs keep up with nutritional and taste trends, and make timely changes in their menus. I remember how happy it made Guests when sushi and wonderful vegetarian dishes were added to the menus and when healthy meal options for children were introduced. And recently Disney announced an initiative that I was involved in before I left the company: new nutritional guidelines that limit calories, fats, and sugars—and will eventually eliminate all added trans fats—in all the food served in the theme parks.

The point is, if you want to be a great leader, you need to stay on top of progress, not become a dinosaur that is hopelessly out of step with the times. That means being voracious in the pursuit of knowledge, paying attention to everything going on around you, and constantly expanding your frame of reference so you can enhance your business with new and better ways of doing things. In other words, you need to stay ahead of the pack. Here's how:

1. Be a knowledge sponge. When asked what he does on an average workday, the legendary investment expert Warren Buffett said he spends most of his time reading—not just corporate reports and business magazines but entire newspapers, books, and other publications. Why? Because his decisions about potential investments are based not just on business news and data but on information about the entire world. This makes perfect sense to me. In my experience, great leaders keep up with what's going on, not only within their own industries but also in the wider world.

Scientific research actually supports that observation. I read an article some time ago that said that people who have a wide range of knowledge and experience are much more successful in their lives. Just last week I saw a study that said that people who read for pleasure tend to be more successful because their reading makes them more creative. At the same time, studies also reveal some data I find alarming: Only 19 percent of adults read a daily newspaper, and the average American male reads only one book for pleasure every three years.

So if you want a competitive edge, read, read, and read some more. Read industry publications, of course, but don't stop there: Read a daily newspaper; subscribe to *Time, Newsweek,* or other newsmagazines; read novels and nonfiction books; surf the Web for blogs or articles in areas of personal interest. If your gut tells you to delve into something, go for it. You'd be surprised how information that may seem unrelated to your work can feed your mind and help you make better decisions. It sure seems to work for Warren Buffett.

Don't stop at the written word. Take advantage of every medium for gathering information: television, radio, movies, pop music, and any other source you can think of. Listening to a radio in your bathroom while you brush your teeth in the morning will put you one step ahead before you even start your day. Watching the news or other informative TV programs in the evening will add knowledge you can actually sleep on. And when you're out and about, whether it's running errands, taking a business trip, or going on a vacation or a family outing, open your ears and your eyes to all kinds of experiences. You never know where your next great idea will come from. As I go about the business of living, I've learned to continually ask myself this question when something catches my eye: "If I were to take this idea and tweak it a bit, could it be applied effectively in my organization or in some other area of my life?"

For instance, a few years ago, when I first saw remote wireless devices being used to speed up the check-in of rental cars at the airport, I thought, "Why can't we use this technology at our resorts?" At about this same time, Al Weiss was challenging us to find a way to eliminate one of the hassles that hotel guests complain about: the front desk check-in process. Seeing the wireless devices in use, I thought, "Why not check in Guests when they're on the bus from the airport so that the minute they arrive they can go straight to their rooms?" The idea has been set in motion, and once it's fully implemented, the added convenience will not only enhance the Guests' experiences but also save Disney a lot of money by cutting down on front-desk labor, money that can be used to enhance the Guest experience in other ways.

Another example of how technological innovations can be creatively adapted in unforeseen ways is Disney's *Magical Express* program, which eliminated another major vacation hassle, dealing with luggage. Under this plan, Guests at Disney hotels are sent bar-coded luggage tags in the mail well before they leave home. Once they check their bags at the airport, they never touch them again until they enter their hotel rooms. Upon arrival at the Orlando airport, they skip past baggage claim and proceed directly to a Disney Welcome Center, where they are greeted and whisked away in a plush motor coach. The service resumes at the end of their vacations. Guests can check their luggage and receive their boarding passes before even leaving their hotel. The cost for this seamless service? Zero! It's free for the Guests, and the return on investment for Disney is incalculable.

Improvements like those are possible only when leaders are open to new knowledge. But too many leaders get motivated to learn only when their business is in decline or in the aftermath of some disaster. When things are going well, they get complacent and start to fall behind the learning curve. So make your mind a sponge in good times as well as bad times, day in and day out, not just when you need to learn something specific.

2. Fill in your gaps. Few leaders are born with the whole package of skills and gifts that they need to achieve greatness. But the smart ones know what they're missing and make an effort to acquire it. One of the seven habits in Stephen R. Covey's hugely popular book *The 7 Habits of Highly Effective People* is called "Sharpen the Saw." What Covey means is: If you want to keep performing better, you need to persistently upgrade your skills and knowledge, just as you need to keep sharpening a saw when you're cutting wood. How sharp is your saw? When was the last time you sharpened it? Remember, it doesn't make sense to sharpen a saw just once unless you plan never to use it again. It should be an ongoing process. If your knowledge is not up-to-date or if you're not as good at some aspect of your work as you could be, you need to sharpen that saw again and again. Chances are you know right now where your weaknesses lie or what you need to improve. If you don't know, ask your manager, a trusted colleague, a friend, or even your spouse or partner, and urge him or her to tell you the truth.

One great way to figure out what you need to learn or improve on is to look at your skills in terms of the four areas of competency I cover in Chapter Four:

✳ Technical competence: Are you expanding and refining your skill base?

✳ Management competence: Are you regularly upgrading your ability to control and organize the environment for maximum efficiency?

✳ Technological competence: Are you keeping up-to-date on ways to adapt technology to do your job faster and cheaper or to improve customer and employee satisfaction?

✳ Leadership competence: Are you continuing to learn more about the fine art of leading others?

Once you identify gaps in your repertoire, take immediate steps to fill them, and go about it energetically, methodically, and diligently. Don't listen to the voice in your head that says you can get by without them or that it's too late in the game and you'll never be able to catch up. I don't know about old dogs, but I can tell you for sure that experienced leaders *can* learn new tricks, and those who create magic are constantly on the lookout for tricks that can give them an edge. Remember, the most important skills are hard before they become easy, so don't shy away from a challenge.

Let me give you a personal example. I used to be terrified of public speaking. In fact, I dropped out of a college speech class the night before my first practice talk because I was so scared I couldn't stop shaking. After the traumatic event, I put all thoughts of public speaking out of my mind. Then, in 1979, when I was thirty-five and was an executive at Marriott, the director of marketing asked me to give a thirty-minute speech to a convention group. I said, "Sure, no problem." But there *was* a problem. Since I had avoided public speaking for so many years, I didn't really know how to do it. So I just wrote out what I wanted to say on a yellow pad and read it, word for word. At one point I glanced up at the audience, and I saw, crystal clear in their eyes, what they were thinking: "Stop! Just stop talking and quit punishing us."

I rambled on for a while longer, and when I finally walked off the stage to some polite clapping, I felt an ache in my stomach that I still feel when I think back to that day. I would have been happy never to give another speech in my life, but I knew I had to learn how to speak effectively if I wanted to advance my career. You simply can't lead if you can't stand before a group and explain your vision in a way that inspires people to do what needs to be done.

So I became determined to acquire that skill. Fortunately, Bill Marriott's father-in-law, Royal Garff, who taught speech at the University of Utah, was willing to spend some time with me. He gave me some of the best advice of my career: (1) don't give speeches, tell stories; (2) use personal examples, whether they're about your family, your dog, or losing your bicycle; (3) never let anyone write a speech for you; and (4) never give a speech about anything you are not passionate about. With his advice in mind, I started practicing on my employees, and after a while I felt comfortable enough to speak to small groups at the charitable organizations I was involved with. Finally, I summoned up the courage to speak to a business group again. It was a big success. I talked about leadership and time management, which, as you can tell from this book, are subjects I'm passionate about, and I made my points with personal examples and family stories.

Over time I got more and more comfortable with public speaking, something that many people (and I was one of them) actually fear more than death. The difference is, you can't learn to avoid death, but you *can* learn to be a good speaker. Now I give speeches to hundreds of people a week, and I can barely keep up with the demand for my lectures. And I'm not only good at it, I love it. Still, my education continues. I watch great speakers and learn from them, and I frequently pick up material for speeches by exposing myself to new information and fresh points of view. Just this year I took a three-day seminar at the Disney Institute to learn how to improve service in health care institutions. I learned so much that I can now speak to health care professionals with confidence and authority.

This brings me to another important piece of advice: Don't just learn things that relate to your current position. Acquire an understanding of your whole business and the industry it's in. You might not need all the information now, but having a wider knowledge base will help you advance to higher positions of leadership, and when you *do* move up and expand your range of concern, you'll be better equipped to lead, teach, and partner with your colleagues. In my case I always worked in operations, but I made a point of learning about sales, marketing, finance, and all the other parts of the business so I could train people better and help other departments execute their responsibilities. And sometimes, what I learned had benefits at home as well as at work.

For example, once, when I felt the need to better understand the chefs who worked for me, I signed up for a course in French cooking. For twelve weeks I devoted a chunk of my Sundays to the course, and I practiced what I learned on my family. As a result of that experience, I not only understood what our chefs needed to do their jobs well but also got to feed my family a lot of delicious meals together (eventually, though, I had to stop cooking before I killed them with all the cream and butter).

3. Master business fundamentals. This is one area of knowledge every leader and every aspiring leader need to study. Even if your current responsibilities don't include managing a budget or justifying a financial statement to stakeholders, someday they probably will. And whatever your position is now, understanding what makes businesses tick will make you a far better leader.

Do you know what your business unit's strategic plan is? Have you looked at your company's annual report? Do you know how to interpret budget statements? Are you familiar with the metrics that drive your business and the measures that drive management decisions? Do you understand what your division or department needs to do to be profitable and how your finances fit with the overall operation? If you don't, go find out, and if you don't understand something, ask someone.

Also, don't just learn about your own company. Study the entire industry and the national and global economies as a whole. If you've never taken Economics 101, sign up for a university extension course. Take a class in finance. Study labor-management issues, and learn how they relate to your industry. Read the business and finance sections of the newspaper every day. Subscribe to *Fortune* or *Forbes* or *BusinessWeek*, or browse such publications online.

4. Learn from the best. Find out who are the best at doing what you do or what your team does, and study them. If, for example, you find it hard to inspire your team, find people who have great reputations as motivators, and observe them in action. Talk to them and to the people on their teams, and find out how they work their magic. And don't just look in the obvious places. Expand beyond your type of business or industry. If you run a supermarket, for example, you might get an idea for a food display by visiting a fancy department store. And vice versa: If you run a clothing shop or a hardware store, go to a gourmet food emporium and get ideas for a merchandise arrangement.

The point is, no matter what business you're in, if it's excellence you're after, you have to know what it looks like, tastes like, sounds like, and feels like. By constantly observing and learning from the best of the best, you will make your own operation better and better. When I was with Marriott, the company was going through a growth period, building larger hotels and moving into the convention, banquet, and meeting business. At the time, our main competition was Hyatt, which had a reputation for operating the most professional banquet and convention services. So I visited several Hyatts to learn what they were doing. I would walk around and take page after page of notes about everything from their silver chafing dishes to their floor layout to the demeanor of their waitstaff.

The next thing I did was call upon the man who had first taught me to learn from the best, Eugene Scanlan, my former boss at another great hotel, the Waldorf-Astoria. Gene was the one who once sent me to six different delicatessens to sample the pastrami, corned beef, coleslaw, potato salad, and pickles so that I could help the Waldorf improve the quality of those items. Now I asked Gene to help me figure out what equipment to purchase for the new J. W. Marriott in Washington, D.C. At his invitation, I spent two days at the Waldorf examining every single piece. With each passing hour I learned more and more about high-quality equipment.

But I wasn't finished. Now that I had all that information, I had to figure out how to best adapt it for our specific needs at Marriott. So I spent almost a year choosing the new equipment to purchase, even visiting manufacturers as far away as Korea to learn what leading companies around the world were using and how it could be customized. By the end of that year, I had become a bona fide expert in banquet serving equipment. As a result, the Washington hotel opened to great success, and I had the pleasure of watching a series of beautiful weddings and elegant corporate meetings with pride.

For the rest of my career, I always told managers to go to the best operations related to their areas of concern and look for better ways of doing things. When I was at Disney World, for instance, I heard that Ritz-Carlton did a great job with valet parking, so I told certain managers to go learn from them. They didn't have to stay overnight, just park their car with the valet, have a drink, use the bathroom, sit in the lobby, or observe the check-in and check-out procedures. Sure enough, they came away with new ideas to implement back in their operations, and not just about parking. They also came away inspired.

Sure, you can glean new ideas by reading trade magazines, going to industry conferences, and the like, and you should absolutely do those things as much as possible. But there is no substitute for hands-on experience. Maybe it's because the mind works in a different way when you're immersed in a real-life environment, but whatever the reason, I always find that the best way to stimulate fresh thinking is to experience the very best. And when you see something interesting, no matter how far removed it may seem from your sphere of business, ask yourself, "How can I adapt that idea to my organization?"

5. Learn from your competitors. You and your company might be good, but so is your opposition. And if it's not, you can learn from it what *not* to do. So keep an eye on *all* your competitors. One day when I was walking around a large convention hotel in Orlando, I ran into the general manager, whom I'd known for a number of years. He asked me what I was doing there. I told him I just wanted to see what my competitors were up to. He was shocked, but I was even more shocked when he said he'd never set foot in a Disney hotel in all the years he'd been managing hotels in the area. I didn't say it, of course, but I thought, "What a wasted opportunity! His lack of curiosity actually gives Disney an edge." A few weeks later, I was invited to a United Way banquet in that same hotel. I accepted immediately; it was a great chance to observe the competition in action. Sure enough, I learned something the minute I arrived. At every door to the ballroom were two or three service personnel, greeting guests and asking if they required special meals. Other servers were already at the tables, pulling out chairs and seating people. At most banquets those employees are hanging out in the kitchen while the guests are arriving. I was so impressed by that simple idea that I went right back to Disney and put it into practice, adding a touch of my own: At the end of our banquets, service personnel would be back at the doors, saying good-bye and thanking the departing guests.

6. Keep up with your colleagues. Someone once told me to get to know a good lawyer and a good doctor long before you need them because when you *do* need them, they'll take much better care of you if you've established a good personal relationship. I took that advice, and I've been getting my annual physical from Dr. Robert Blee in Washington, D.C., for twenty-eight years. We're growing old together in good health because I trust him implicitly, and I'm more than willing to pay the cost of an airline ticket to see him once a year. He knows everything about me, from my family's medical history to exactly what I weighed back in 1980, and he takes whatever time he needs to give me new ideas for maintaining my health. And he has lots of ideas because he's a smart professional who keeps up with developments in his field.

I feel the same way about my professional colleagues. In fact, I'm certain that the main reason my new public speaking and consulting business is doing so well is that I maintained solid relationships with a network of people I met during my years in the hospitality industry. When I started my business after retiring from Disney, I had more than twelve hundred contacts in my database. And they're not just names of people I may have met once; I've had contact with most of them a few times a year and done favors for some of them along the way. Once they were in a position to help me with ideas and advice in getting my business off the ground, they were happy to do so, and the education they continue to provide is enormously helpful. That's the power of relationships.

Cultivating professional contacts is like going to a lifelong school with a brilliant faculty you can always turn to for knowledge. Consider it a professional necessity to form good relationships with as many people in your field as possible, and stay in touch with them as you—and they—move from one position or organization to another. Sure, it's easy to find excuses not to attend an industry conference or a trade show: You're busy, you'd rather be with your family, travel is tiresome, and so forth. Too many leaders send their junior colleagues to these events instead of taking the time to go themselves, and that can be a big mistake. It's not just that you'll miss out on learning opportunities but that you'll lose touch with human beings you stand to learn from in the future.

Throughout my time at Disney World, whenever I saw that an interesting conference or trade show was coming to Orlando—and sometimes even to New York, Chicago, Atlanta, or other accessible locations—I'd note it in my Day-Timer and try to make arrangements, months in advance, to attend. Inevitably, on the day I was supposed to leave for one of these events, I'd have the urge to cancel because I was so busy. But in the end I was almost always glad I went because I solidified existing relationships and added names to my list of colleagues. Here are two tips to help you overcome the urge to bow out of these events: (1) Schedule them on your calendar, and (2) buy nonrefundable airline tickets.

7. Study your customer base. Do you know what the most frequently asked question at Walt Disney World is? No, it's not "Where is the nearest bathroom?" or "How do I get to the Magic Kingdom?" It's "What time is the three o'clock parade?" You read that right: "What time is the three o'clock parade?" But it's not a gag question, like "Who is buried in Grant's tomb?" What the Guests *really* mean when they ask the question is: "What time does the three o'clock parade get to this location?" Because Disney leaders and Cast Members know their Guests so well, everyone is trained to expect the question, and no one laughs when it comes up. Instead, everyone will say something like "It passes by here at twelve minutes after three, and if you stand right over there, your child will have a great view of Cinderella."

It's obvious that leaders need to know their customers. But *what* they need to know isn't always obvious. This is where customer surveys and other kinds of market research are vital, but that's not enough. Your customers are human beings, and you need to know what makes them tick. At Disney we call this Guestology.

Guestology is the study of what Guests like and don't like, as well as what they want and don't want. As I've mentioned in earlier chapters, this information is gathered in a number of different ways. Questionnaires are administered both on-site and over the Internet. Comment surveys are collected throughout the property. Cast Members gather verbal opinions as they interact with Guests, and they report significant findings to managers. But that's not all. Disney also studies hard data related to preferences and patterns such as crowd flow, transportation use, occupancy rates, and other important factors, so resources can be deployed efficiently. In addition, trained experts conduct focus groups of eight to ten volunteer Guests to gather feedback on specific issues that are under evaluation, whether it's the healthy meals for children or the FASTPASS® system. Face-to-face interviews are conducted in resort lobbies and park exits, asking Guests about their experiences that very day, so problems can be fixed before the sun comes up the next morning. If, for example, a significant percentage of Guests say that the restrooms were not as clean as they should be or that the check-in process at their resorts took too long, the information goes straight to the appropriate managers for immediate corrective action. In all, more than a million Guests a year are surveyed, and the information leads to continuous improvements in service.

Don't let the term fool you. You don't have to run a hotel or resort to practice Guestology. After all, the purpose is to gather accurate, reliable information in order to provide better products and services, and that's something every business needs to do. So take advantage of every method available for gathering information about your customer base. And be sure to make the results of your research available to everyone in your organization.

8. Follow the compass. At Walt Disney World, Guestology combines demographics with psychographics. The former gives you measurable facts about your customers, like where they come from, how they travel, how big their families are, and so forth; the latter tells you who those customers really are. At Disney, psychographics is the holy grail of research, and it's broken down into four parts, called compass points: needs, wants, stereotypes, and emotions. What do people who plan a trip to Disney World need? A vacation. What do those vacationing Guests want? Lots of things, of course, but mostly they want fun, hassle-free trips and memories to last a lifetime. What stereotypes or preconceived notions do they bring with them? Research reveals positive ones such as clean facilities, friendly people, and fun-filled days, as well as negatives such as long lines and high prices. And what emotions do Guests experience when they're at Disney World? Common responses include excitement, thrills, and tiredness at the end of the day.

What are the needs, wants, stereotypes, and emotions *your* customers bring to their interactions with your organization? In order to stay ahead of the pack, I strongly suggest that you devote whatever time and resources you need to find out. You can fill in the four compass points regardless of the business you're in. If you're in health care, for instance, your customers' basic need is medical care; the wants are probably to get well and to have pain-free experiences; the negative stereotypes you have to overcome are that it's a cold, unfriendly environment, with a chance of medical mistakes; and the emotions they come with include hope as well as fear of the unknown and fear of pain. By filling in the data on all four compass points, you will come away with a clear understanding of your customers, and you can gear your hiring, your training, and your processes and systems toward exceeding their expectations.

9. Expand your horizons. In November 1985 I was promoted to vice president, food and beverage planning, for all Marriott

Hotels and Resorts. This job, which entailed traveling to facilities all over the globe, left me with lasting impressions that changed the way I saw both the world in general and my work in particular. When I was in Mexico to do research on two hotel projects, I spent most of three days being driven around by a man who did not speak a word of English. Since I spoke about three words of Spanish at the time, we could hardly use language to communicate. So we bonded by showing each other pictures of our sons, and somehow we accomplished our work of examining competing hotels and restaurants to give me an understanding of the products and services that were important in Mexico. And we had a great time together. It was a lesson I was able to generalize to all kinds of business situations in the future: There is always common ground if you look for it.

I learned a lot of other lessons in the years I crisscrossed the globe for Marriott. Perhaps the most important part of my curriculum was the exposure to ethnic, cultural, racial, and religious diversity. I found out quickly that human beings everywhere are basically the same: We're all trying to have decent lives and to make things better for our families, and we're all proud of our cultures and countries. We can read all about our common humanity, and we can feel passionately about it, but experiencing it firsthand moves that knowledge from the brain to the heart and into the bloodstream. It changed the way I was to treat diversity issues in the workplace for the rest of my career.

In my travels I also acquired specific knowledge about the business I was in, and that helped equip me for my next job, as general manager of a hotel. I had never managed a hotel before, but I had checked into and out of more hotel rooms all over the world than I could count, and I had enjoyed some of the best hotel services in the world as a guest. You just don't get that education in a classroom. As a result, I quickly made changes that

I knew from personal experience guests would appreciate. I kept the health club open twenty-four hours a day because I'd seen firsthand that travelers often have to work out very early or very late. I added a sundries counter to the end of the front desk because I'd been frustrated when the shops were closed and I couldn't get things I needed. I put coffee in the rooms and installed an express buffet breakfast because I knew that business travelers are always in a hurry in the morning. And I put full-size ironing boards in the rooms because I had experienced how annoying it was to iron on one of those miniature boards. While all these enhancements are common in hotels today, they were rarities when I put them into practice more than twenty years ago.

That's what expanding your frame of reference does; it opens your eyes to better ways of doing things. But you don't necessarily have to fly all over the world to enlarge your frame of reference. You can do it anywhere, as long as you're open to trying new things and going to unfamiliar places. Drive a different route to and from work so you can see other neighborhoods. Take your family to a different kind of restaurant, and order something you've never tasted. Watch the Discovery Channel or The Learning Channel or public television instead of your usual programs. Rent some foreign films. If you have kids, listen to some of the music they're into or browse their textbooks. When was the last time you went to a museum? I hadn't been to one in a long time, and when Priscilla dragged me to an opening one night, the last thing on my mind was finding business ideas. But seeing the exhibits actually gave me ideas for making the food buffets and centerpieces at Disney World a lot more interesting and attractive. For instance, in one restaurant we did away with chafing dishes and cooked the food at cooking stations made of brick and other rustic materials, right in front of our Guests.

Where did I get that idea, which became a big hit? From a painting of a cowboy cooking over an open fire.

The point is, wherever you go and whatever you do, *pay attention*. There are many ways to gather information besides crunching numbers and reading reports. Coming up with great ideas is like going fishing: The wider you cast your net, the better your chances of hooking some good ones. So expand your horizons, and always keep your eyes and ears open. Soon you will begin to find inspiration everywhere—from commuter trains to city parks to hair salons to supermarkets, even to the shop where you get your car's oil changed.

10. Keep the people you lead ahead of the pack. You're not the only one who has to stay on the leading edge of the learning curve. As I've said, one of a leader's most vital responsibilities is to support the ongoing education of his or her team members, so encourage yours to stretch beyond the usual training they need on their career paths. Send them to conferences and seminars, recommend books, suggest places to go and people to meet, and instill in them the habit of noticing their surroundings as they go about their lives. You might even take them to places yourself, the way Disney's senior vice president of operations Don Robinson once took several general managers to some of the best hotels in Asia. He had them personally experience the highest level of service from the guest's point of view, and they returned to Orlando with an enlarged sense of what is possible.

Make sure your direct reports know that you consider learning one of their responsibilities, and find ways to expose them to great ideas and living examples of excellence. This concept is an integral part of the Disney culture, and it has led to some spectacularly profitable ideas—like pin trading, for example.

In 1998, George Kalogridis, who was then VP of Epcot, traveled to the winter Olympics in Nagano, Japan, with two of his colleagues to check out an exhibit that we thought could be adapted for use at Disney World. The Disney delegation liked the exhibit, but what really caught its attention were the hundreds of people trading Olympic pins. Because the traders were from all over the world, most of them couldn't speak one another's languages, but they were communicating perfectly through facial expressions and hand signals. And they weren't trading just official Olympic pins but also corporate pins made by companies like IBM, Coca-Cola, and Kodak.

The rest is business history. The next year, when the millennium celebration opened at Epcot, our stores were stockpiled with pins of our own. That year, Disney sold about three million dollars' worth of pins. And that was just the beginning; seeing how popular the pins were, I started wearing a pin-covered lanyard as I walked around Disney World. Well, pretty soon just about everyone else, including many of the Guests, was sporting a lanyard. The little idea that our alert travelers had brought back from the Olympics became an integral part of the culture. Wildly popular with everyone from Guests to Cast Members to Disney shareholders, pin sales now amount to many millions of dollars a year, and there's no end in sight. And by the way, the pin-trading phenomenon is what gave me the idea to create special recognition pins for our Cast Members. Just goes to show how great ideas can spark other great ideas.

Before I close this chapter, I want to comment on the leadership work the U.S. Army is doing to stay ahead of the pack. I have for many years worked closely with many organizations and their leaders, but few have been as impressive as the army. It continually brings in leaders from the corporate and non-profit worlds to help it find ways to adapt the best leadership practices to its needs. It does this for the same reason you should do it: to keep ahead by learning better ways to lead in this diverse, ever-changing world. The army has a very clear mission statement: "To provide to the country leaders of character, to serve the common defense." This is its reason for being, and it clearly understands that in order to be successful, it must prepare its personnel at every level to lead us in these uncertain times. Your organization can do the same.

In this fast-changing world, it's important for leaders to always keep up with new information and cultural trends, and to always keep their eyes, ears, and minds open for fresh ways of doing things. Remember the old song "Breaking Up Is Hard to Do"? Well, *keeping* up is hard to do too. But it's also exhilarating. Besides, you *have* to do it because, well, think of the alternative. After all, if you don't keep up, you fall behind, and if you fall *too* far behind, you might get so lost that no one can find you.

ACTION STEPS

 ✳ Stay current with industry and business trends as well as cultural trends and social movements.

 ✳ Find out what the most cutting-edge services and products are.

 ✳ Expose yourself to the best; reflect on your experience, then act on it.

 ✳ Go on "best-practice trips" to learn from companies with great reputations.

* Keep up with the changes in your industry by going to the right meetings, reading the right journals, and knowing the right people.

* Forge strong professional relationships; get to know the experts, and stay in touch with them on an ongoing basis.

* Practice your own version of Guestology by developing methods for learning what makes your customers tick.

* Consistently ask your employees what the organization can do better.

* Expand your frame of reference by trying new things every chance you get.

* Surf the Internet for new ideas.

* Aggressively solicit information about the services and products your competitors offer.

* Encourage your team members to always keep their eyes and ears open—in the workplace and beyond—and publicly recognize their contributions.

CHAPTER ELEVEN

STRATEGY #9

BE CAREFUL WHAT YOU SAY AND DO

One morning early in my career as an executive, Priscilla said to me as I left for work, "Lee, be careful what you say and do today. They're watching you and judging you." Her insight had a huge impact on me; from that day forward, I followed her advice. Every morning I drove to work, parked my car, took a deep breath, and worked hard at behaving like a true professional all day long. I've been quoting Priscilla ever since. In fact, I believe it might be the best advice any leader can get.

Like parents, whose every word and action are lessons to their children, leaders have to model appropriate behavior at all times. Whether we like it or not, we're always being watched and evaluated, and we're always teaching—not just when we're giving speeches or running meetings, but also when we're walking down hallways, or leaving parking lots, or talking on cell phones to our kids. That is why we have to conduct ourselves impeccably at all times. "When you arrive at work," I always tell other leaders, "imagine a big red curtain opening. You are now onstage!" So perform like a professional, and like a good Broadway show, you'll have a long, successful run; behave unprofessionally, and your career will flop.

There is a crucial difference between being a professional and *being* professional. What do I mean? Well, all doctors, lawyers, CEOs, and so on are professionals, but many of them behave in ways that are *un*professional, while an awful lot of mail room clerks, receptionists, and truck drivers are consummate professionals. In other words, professionalism is not defined by job title. Nor is it only a matter of competence; you can do a decent job and still not be a true professional. As we'll see, true professionalism is mainly about attitude and demeanor and the image you project to the world.

At the end of the day, there are no untold stories. If you're a leader, the stories that are told about you matter a great deal because they determine your reputation, and, as my mother used to say, "You have to protect your reputation because it's the only one you have." When your reputation is tarnished, you lose your credibility, and when your credibility goes, you lose the one thing leaders need most: the trust of the people you lead. Remember also that you have a different reputation with every person who knows you. Work hard to make each one a good one.

True professionals demonstrate with their actions that they are trustworthy. That's why it's important to take charge of your own narrative; if you don't write your own story, the people around you will fill in the blanks. One way to think about your professional image is this: If you were a brand, what product or service would you want to resemble? I always want my brand to be like Lexus—dependable, sturdy, efficient, a consistently high-level performer, even when it has a lot of miles on it. After all, I'm still driving my old reliable 1993 Lexus because I never have to worry about its performing.

What does your brand stand for? Excellence? Integrity? Reliability? Professionals stand for all those qualities and more—and they personify them every minute of their working lives. Here are some guidelines for becoming a consummate professional.

1. Demonstrate a passionate commitment to your role. Passion may contribute more to the greatness of a leader than any other trait. It is the driving force that enables people to attain far more than they ever imagined. Passion energizes your body, focuses your mind, and sets fire to your heart. And it's contagious. People fall in line behind passionate leaders because they get ignited by the same sense of purpose. After all, you can't lead if no one follows you, and if you're not passionate about achieving your objectives, no one will want to march in your parade.

I'm proud to say that once the Great Leader Strategies took hold at *Walt Disney World*® Resort, we saw passion on display day after day, in the faces of everyone from frontline Cast Members to the highest executive ranks. They didn't just like their work; they *loved* their work. They didn't just care about doing a good job; they were dedicated to it. Everyone cared deeply about what he or she did every day, and that translated into a commitment to performance excellence.

True professionals love what they do so much that they get up in the morning inspired by the work that awaits them and eager to tackle the challenges of the day. Their enthusiasm, their upbeat optimism, and their pride in what they contribute to their companies and their communities inspire others to achieve a level of excellence that they often didn't even know they had in them. My rule of thumb for leaders who wonder if they're in the right position is this: You should feel as excited about going to work in the morning as you are about getting home at night. If you find that you're not inspired to start new projects or take bold initiatives, and you're starting to go home earlier and earlier, it might be time to rethink your situation. Looking back on my career, I realize that the only times I actively sought a different position was when I started to feel a loss of passion. And I can say with complete honesty that when I worked at Disney World, I was happy to get up at 5:00 A.M. knowing I'd be creating magic all day.

At the same time, professionals understand the risk of burnout and imbalance, so they spend exactly as much time at work as they need to get the job done right—not a minute more and not a minute less. Many people talk about having a business life and a personal life, but in reality you have only one life, and the best leaders are passionate about everything in it.

2. Do what it takes to get the job done. Committed professionals do whatever is necessary to do the job right. This might mean going to work on a Saturday or Sunday, or staying into the night if necessary. In a crisis it could mean working day and night seven days a week. Basically, it means being fully present whenever and wherever your leadership, experience, and professional expertise are required. Plus it means devoting time to improving your skills, doing research, taking trips, and all the other extras I've mentioned in previous chapters so you can know what's going on, develop relationships, and stay ahead of the pack. And for leaders, it also means inspiring others to do the same. Remember, those you lead are always watching, and if they see you doing whatever it takes to get the job done, they will follow your example.

When I became general manager of the Springfield Marriott, I quickly learned that when the majority of your guests are business travelers, most of your problems crop up in the evening and early in the morning. That's because most business travelers arrive between 4:00 P.M. and 8:00 P.M. and check out before 9:00 A.M. So I made sure to arrive at work before most of the guests woke up. That covered the morning problems, but since I could not work both days and nights, I needed mature, experienced leadership on hand during those crucial evening hours. Soon enough it became clear that the current resident manager, Doreen Robinson, would be a perfect fit. I had watched Doreen carefully, and it was obvious that she knew the guests and the hotel better than anyone else, including even me.

The problem was, she liked her daytime hours. I could have settled for someone else; there were reasonable candidates at the hotel, and I could have recruited someone from another Marriott. But both my brain and my gut were adamant: Doreen was the one for the job. I had no money to entice her with, and I could not create a new position with a more prestigious title. But I could appeal to her professionalism. I told her that I was the general manager during the day, and I needed her to be the equivalent of general manager at night. I acknowledged that the change in schedule would be a sacrifice for her but promised that the assignment would last only a few months, during which time we would train the evening managers to handle more responsibilities. I also pointed out that it would be a valuable learning experience for her, just as working odd shifts had proved to be for me early in my career, and that new experiences can be more important to a career in the long run than added compensation.

It didn't take much convincing; being the consummate professional that she was, Doreen recognized that by working those evening hours, she would be making an extremely valuable contribution to the goals we'd set for the hotel, and that it might prove beneficial to her career as well. She rose to the occasion, and I had peaceful evenings and sound sleep because I had 100 percent trust in her judgment and her strong commitment to the business. And the temporary sacrifice did pay off for her; she went on to become the director of human resources, a position that gave her life more balance and utilized her excellent people skills to the benefit of the entire hotel staff. In fact, I heard from her just recently; she's still in Springfield, making magic for her Marriott associates.

3. Set high standards. Professionals continuously raise the bar and help those they lead leap over it. But that's not all. By setting higher and higher performance expectations, they inspire the people they lead to set even higher standards for themselves. At the same time, they are not unrealistic; their standards are lofty but reachable, and they hold people accountable for reaching them because they're all about performance and results. So, as I mentioned earlier, make sure you're crystal clear about what each person's responsibility is, what his or her authority is, and what he or she will be held accountable for. Tell the people you lead exactly what will happen if they don't meet performance standards, and be prepared to help poor performers get better.

I remember a couple of early lessons given to me by Alice and J. Willard Marriott, the cofounders of the Marriott Corporation. On one occasion Mrs. Marriott told me, "Lee, if you don't improve the food in this restaurant, I am going to take my name off it." But she didn't stop there; she took the time to teach me how to make a good chili, starting with pinto beans instead of kidney beans, because she cared deeply about the company.

Her husband, J. Willard, did too. One day in 1975 he pointed to my nametag, which read, "Lee Cockerell, Restaurant Manager," and said, "Cockerell, are you the manager here?" I said, "Yes, sir." He said, "Then why don't you get a haircut and look like it?" That was the last day I had the faddish long hair of the seventies. I learned that fads and professionalism don't always go hand in hand. And I learned something even more important: Mr. and Mrs. Marriott cared enough for their company, and for me, to be candid and clear about their standards, and that's what leaders have to do.

More important, professional leaders serve as role models by setting high standards for *themselves* and holding themselves publicly accountable for meeting them. Earlier I mentioned how as a hotel manager I used to place gold stickers on the restaurant menus, inviting guests to come to me if they were ever unhappy with their experience. Well, this didn't just help me learn what was and wasn't working in the restaurant, it also improved the overall service dramatically. Why? Because in seeing the high standard I had set for myself, the rest of the staff raised their own standards as well. I also posted a sign for hotel employees, inviting them to call me twenty-four hours a day if they were concerned about safety issues that their managers were not addressing. I never received a call, because the signs themselves raised the bar on safety standards, and the managers in turn became more responsive to employee concerns.

4. Have a positive attitude. You'll never hear a true professional whine, complain, or make excuses. You'll never see one mope, or act pessimistic or hopeless. It's not that he or she is in denial when things aren't going well; professionals are always grounded in reality, and while they can be visionaries, their visions are fact-based. But even when there are challenges to overcome, their attitude is always positive, and they never stop looking for solutions to problems that other people would give up on. If you want to see true professionalism in action, watch how some of the best football coaches act when their teams are hopelessly behind. They roam the sidelines, lifting chins and bucking up spirits; they try new approaches and call out new plays; and they never let their players get away with giving anything less than their best.

It's important for you as a leader to display a positive attitude at all times, because you set the mood for your team or organization. In my career, I've learned never to underestimate the immense power of a smile; you can't imagine the impact it has on the people who look to you for leadership. Sure, it's not always easy to remember to smile in the midst of a busy and challenging workday. But think of the message you give out if you walk around with a frown or a scowl on your face or focus your worried eyes on the ground. Like great parents, great leaders don't wear the effects of bad days in front of others. It not only hurts your reputation but triggers worry and fear among your employees, rather than optimism.

Modeling a positive attitude doesn't stop with just your facial expressions and your demeanor. You should also be upbeat and positive in your dialogue with others. Professionals simply do not speak in a negative way about their colleagues or companies, and they don't succumb to petty gossip. Wherever you work, you're bound to see process problems, structural flaws, and all too human shortcomings. By all means, identify them, speak out about them, and make recommendations for fixing them. But *don't* sit around moaning or complaining to people who can't do anything about the situation. Instead, take appropriate action, and do it with an upbeat attitude. I guarantee that others will notice and follow your example in their dealings as well. Like passionate commitment to your work, a positive attitude is contagious.

5. Look and carry yourself like a professional. Every business and every workplace has a certain appearance code, whether it's a matter of explicit policy or an unstated part of the culture. At Disney World, for instance, Cast Members know before they start their first day of work that they're expected to conform to a certain standard of grooming regarding not just their costumes but also their hair, tattoos, body piercings, and so on. True professionals not only adhere to the customs of their environments but do so with impeccable care.

Still, if you want to be seen as a professional, it's not enough to dress professionally; you have to pay close attention to your entire demeanor. This means watching your posture, your mannerisms, and your facial expressions. It also means keeping your behavior under control at all times. Make sure never to lose your temper or blow your cool; when something goes wrong, find other ways to vent your frustration. As Priscilla wisely said, people are always watching, so the show must go on, no matter what you feel inside. You have to give a great performance at all times so people will want to be around you, follow you, and learn from you.

6. Be a full-time professional—even when the curtain is down. True professionals do the right thing in the right way, even when no one is watching. That means all the time; you can't be a part-time professional, and you can't act professionally only when you are in the spotlight.

I learned this firsthand when I worked at the Philadelphia Marriott. Periodically, executives from corporate headquarters, including the CEO, Bill Marriott, paid us a visit on relatively short notice. Every time one of those VIP visits was announced, my whole staff ran around frantically to get ready for inspection. This struck me as not only wasteful but dishonest and unprofessional. Why should we have to get ready for a special visitor when the place should be ready *all the time*? After all, Bill Marriott made those surprise visits for that very reason; he wanted areas of the hotel that the guests never saw to be just as clean and organized as the public areas. So I changed the policy: Everything was to be maintained so well that we would be proud to show it off to anyone at any time. From then on, the place always looked as it did when we were waiting for a carload of VIPs to arrive.

Remember, the people you lead are not only watching how you act, but also looking at your surroundings and judging you by what they see. You might want to do an exercise that the Disney Institute uses in its training programs; it's one that anyone in any business can try. Just close your eyes and imagine coming to your workplace as if you were a visitor or a customer. As you visualize the scene, what do you see? Does the area look inviting and clean? Do the employees look focused or distracted? Engaged or bored? Passionate or uninvolved? Remember, professionals are always conscious of sending the right message, not only in their appearance and demeanor but in their environments as well. Everything speaks.

7. Model personal ownership. Taking ownership means always being accountable for everything that goes on in your organization, even if it is not strictly your responsibility. At Disney the attitude of personal ownership has been part of the company culture ever since Walt created his first theme park. For example, everyone—from souvenir salespeople to upper management—is accountable for keeping every inch of the parks and resorts spotless. As a result, it is so commonplace for Cast Members to bend down and pick up trash as they go about their jobs that the action took on a name, the Disney Scoop. And I'll never forget how pleased I once was to hear one of the housekeepers refer to the rooms she prepared for arriving Guests as "my rooms." She was a professional who took pride in cleaning those rooms as if they were her very own. So, whatever your current position is, take personal ownership for everything in your organization, and teach those you lead to do the same.

8. Don't lose your sense of humor. Knowing that joy brings out the best in people and that tension does not, professionals try to lighten up the workplace. They are earnest but not somber, single-minded in pursuit of results but not grim. Professionals take their work very seriously, but they don't take *themselves* too seriously. Supremely confident and comfortable in their skins, they have no need to posture or preen or show off their status. They enjoy seeing people have fun, as long as the work gets done.

So use humor to find ways to liven up the workplace and break the monotony for the people you lead. Create surprises. Make jokes. Believe me, I may have worked in "the happiest place on earth," but it's not always a barrel of laughs to run a huge operation. Behind the scenes, Disney World might have been as grim as any office complex or factory floor if the leaders didn't make a priority of lightening things up. Sometimes, Cinderella, Mickey Mouse, or some other Disney character would pop up unexpectedly at a workshop or the call center to put a smile on Cast Members' faces. Or an executive might wander around the workplace dressed as George Washington on Presidents' Day, or Santa Claus at Christmastime, just to get a laugh. I always told our leaders, "If we're not having fun, we can't be doing our best work."

Take your responsibilities seriously, but not *so* seriously that work becomes drudgery. Don't fall prey to the outdated notion that managers have to keep workers' noses to the grindstone in order to get a decent day's work out of them. It's just not true; they'll be far more productive if you create an atmosphere that allows them to leave work with smiles on their faces and maybe even a funny story to share with their families. One day at Disney, I asked Rilous Carter, one of our executives, what would cause him to leave the company. He replied, "When it's not fun anymore." He's not the only one who feels that way.

9. Be a great partner. Professionals know that one big difference between those who get great results and those who fail, and between leaders who leave behind positive legacies and those who exit to sighs of relief, is being able to partner effectively with others. Partnering doesn't come naturally to everyone, but true professionals make a point of cultivating the skills I'm about to describe.

For one, professionals are available when their partners need to see them. They return phone calls and e-mails promptly, and they get back to people quickly with answers to their questions. They welcome input and constructive feedback, and they're humble enough to ask their partners for help when they need it. In turn they are generous with their time and expertise. And most important, they live up to every commitment they make.

Working with Al Weiss at Disney for thirteen years taught me the true meaning of a professional partnership. I learned early on that he was a trustworthy partner, and I think he knew that about me as well. One big reason we partnered so well was that we kept each other up-to-date and completely informed about everything, good and bad, through personal meetings, e-mail, voice mail, and even notes I slipped under Al's office door from time to time. But here's the main reason Al was a great partner: Like all true professionals, he respected and cared about people on a personal level. I learned he was that kind of partner early on, when one day I told him I wanted to cancel a meeting because my wife was sick and I had to pick up our granddaughter at school. Al said he'd be very upset with me if I *didn't* cancel the meeting and go home because Priscilla was my partner too.

True professionals also avoid the common temptation to compete with their partners instead of really collaborating with them. They work to establish harmonious relationships and to keep those relationships from turning adversarial. Early in my career at Marriott, I learned that lesson the hard way when I was passed over for a promotion to senior vice president of food and beverage because I had made adversaries of three of the vice presidents, and their votes made the difference. The disappointment was a major wake-up call. I'll always be glad that I found the courage and professionalism to repair my relationships with those VPs because if I hadn't, my career might have taken an entirely different course. From that point on, I also worked hard not to create adversaries in the first place, even when I was forced to partner with people I didn't necessarily respect or trust.

Of course, conflicts and differences of opinion are inevitable in business. Professionals keep a sharp eye out for the warning signs and move quickly to resolve tensions and restore trust by finding solutions that satisfy everyone concerned. They also choose their battles wisely; they don't waste their time on petty disagreements and annoyances, but rather save their energy for issues that have real consequences. I remember the time a higher-ranking executive called me in to see him because he was unhappy with a decision I had made that affected his area of responsibility. Even after I explained the reasoning behind my decision in detail, he still disagreed, but to his great credit he said he would give me the benefit of the doubt and let the decision stand. He could have asserted his authority and overruled me, but he didn't. Why? Because he and I had established a strong and trusting partnership over the course of time, and he was placing our relationship, and the good of the company, ahead of his ego. That's how professionals behave.

10. Stay humble. I always loved being a leader. I loved making my influence felt and using my authority to accomplish results. But I learned along the way that great leaders are also great followers. They know when to point the way and when to step aside. No matter how high up in the company or corporation they may be, true professionals are always respectful of people who have more authority and responsibility than they do, and everyone with less. They are consummate team players who know how to put team goals ahead of their personal desires.

I recently participated in a leadership seminar with Jim Collins, the author of *Good to Great*, whose research and writing have made a huge impact on the way business leaders think. Jim said that a key behavior trait of the best leaders is humility. In his extensive research he found that great leaders—the people he calls Level 5 leaders—are ambitious, but ambitious for the work they do, not for personal gain. They worry a whole lot more about their mission and the people they work with than they do about themselves and their stock options.

In other words, professionals never let their egos get in the way of what's best for the organization. Just because you like being in charge doesn't mean you always *should* be in charge, and just because you like having things your way doesn't mean you *should* have everything your way. True professionals have an inner gyroscope that enables them to strike the right balance between bold self-confidence and humility. They project strength and confidence without crossing the line into arrogance or self-importance. If you want to be a professional, you have to cultivate that balancing mechanism, or else you won't know when to assert yourself and when to defer to others.

Sometimes in a crisis a leader simply has to take over and rely on command and control strategies. But the worst thing you can do in tough times is be the boss for the sake of being the boss—especially when there are competent people around who know things you don't. Professionals care more about the outcome than about their image. Ironically, by knowing when to be humble, they end up being even more admired as strong leaders. At Disney, after 9/11, for instance, I stepped back and let Karl Holz and Erin Wallace take center stage and direct the show. As head of Disney World Operations, I was senior to both of them, but they had the expertise we needed at that time, and my job as a professional was to empower them to do what they do best. I believe that the three of us did a great job of leading the operations team through some very difficult times because we saw ourselves as partners and not as a boss and subordinates.

Humility is a key ingredient in professionalism, but it doesn't always come easily to leaders—not at work anyway. At home, if you're lucky, you'll have someone like my wife to remind you where your authority ends. Priscilla would give me this sweet reminder from time to time: "You are not an executive vice president around here." But at work, where you are recognized as a leader, you have to be vigilant at keeping your ego in check. Try using my mantra: "You're never as good as you think you are." I learned that phrase from Kevin Myers, who runs all of Disney's resort operations. Kevin is one of the quietest and most effective executives I ever worked with, and one reason he does such a superb job is that he is humble enough to never be satisfied with what he's accomplished; he is always looking for ways to make the resorts better.

Not every professional is a leader, and not every leader is a true professional. But if you want to be a *great* leader, you have to look, feel, and behave professionally at every moment of every day. Let my wife's wisdom guide you, as it has guided me. Behave as if you're always onstage, because in a way, you are.

ACTION STEPS

✳ Always display passion and commitment.

✳ Be excited about coming to work every day, and share that enthusiasm with your employees.

✳ Spend the right amount of time on the job, doing the right things in the right ways.

✳ Maintain a positive attitude, and make it contagious.

✳ Create strong partnerships, and always be available when your partners need you.

✳ Set the bar high, and personally live up to every standard you set.

✳ Make a good impression through your demeanor, appearance, and environment.

✳ Find ways to break the monotony and routine for people.

✳ Work toward making partners out of your adversaries, and always take the first step.

✳ Focus on collaboration rather than conflict in problem solving.

✳ Know when to step back and let others lead.

✳ Be a role model for professionalism. And remember, you are always onstage!

CHAPTER TWELVE

STRATEGY #10

DEVELOP CHARACTER

My father-in-law, Charles N. Payne, was a rear admiral in the U.S. Navy. When I asked him when he first knew that he was willing to die for his country, he said it was on the day he joined the service and swore to defend the United States Constitution. Then he added something I've never forgotten: "Lee, you have to decide what you stand for long before an incident happens, so you'll be ready to react appropriately." I have found this to be true for leaders in every realm. As a leader you are confronted with difficult moral or ethical decisions every day. You have to know what you stand for and be ready to do the right thing.

This chapter is about character. The word has many meanings, but when we say someone has character, we usually mean that he or she has moral and ethical strength. Great leaders not only have the skills, attitudes, and behavioral traits I've discussed so far but also shine with character. What do you stand for? What are your core values? Where do you draw your lines in the sand? If you want to be a great leader, you not only need to know the answers to those questions but communicate them to the people you lead and reinforce them in every word you speak and every action you take. Frances Hesselbein, the president and chairman of the Leader to Leader Institute, says it this way in her book *Hesselbein on Leadership:* "Leadership is a matter of how to be, not how to do."

I often think there should be a code of ethics for business leaders, as there are for lawyers or doctors. I'm not just talking about obvious rules like not cooking the books or lying to shareholders; we already have laws for such things. I mean standards of professional behavior, the business equivalent of the Hippocratic oath with its famous beginning, "First do no harm," because managers who humiliate, mistreat, and abuse their employees do harm not just to their companies but to society as a whole. But we don't yet have a universal code for business leaders, so we each have to determine our own personal set of values. The following sections will help you identify yours.

1. Anticipate ethical dilemmas. I thought of my father-in-law's advice one day in 1972, when my own character as an executive was put to the test for the first time. I had recently been made the executive assistant manager of the Hilton Hotel in Tarrytown, New York, when the owner of a local taxicab company came into my office and handed me an envelope. In it were ten hundred-dollar bills. "All you have to do to keep that envelope," he said, "is to make sure that my cabs are the only ones that can wait for guests in front of the hotel." My stomach started churning, my body temperature went up a few degrees, and my face flushed. I had never seen a thousand dollars at one time in my life, and I sure could have used it, as Priscilla and I were short on money and struggling to raise our two-year-old son. In those days a thousand bucks could go a long way. But as much as we needed the money, I knew right away what I had to do. I immediately handed the envelope back. I knew what my values were, and I knew then, as I do today, what lines I was not willing to cross.

I was very glad that I had come to grips with my own ethical standards before I was handed that envelope. Make sure that you have too, because it's only a matter of time before you are put in a position, either in business or in your personal life, that will involve making a difficult choice. The front page of the newspaper is full of stories about people who have not prepared themselves for that moment. One way of defining what your own ethical standards are is to ask yourself what you would do in a number of delicate situations. For instance:

* What would you do if you had a chance to take a little money, or some merchandise, from your organization without anyone's finding out and you knew that others were doing it?

* What would you do if your boss told you to inflate the inventory to make your profit margin look higher?

* What would you do if a coworker asked you to do a favor for a friend or family member and it was against company policy?

* What would you do if you knew that a coworker had a drug problem?

* What would you do if you knew that coworkers were abusing their discount privileges or using the mail room to send personal packages?

Ask yourself these kinds of questions and any others that might be relevant to your business or your organization. Anticipating moral and ethical dilemmas and knowing how you'll respond will prepare you to do the right thing if a situation does arise.

2. Live your values. Great leaders not only know what their values are but allow those values to guide their every decision. At *Walt Disney World®* Resort, Cast Members are expected to follow seven core values, and every leader works hard to make those values a living reality. Those core values are as follows:

* **Honesty: We deal with one another in a straightfor-ward manner.** Honesty is the key building block of trust. It applies not only to the ethics of doing business but also to the ways in which people within a team or a company relate to one another. When you think about it, honesty can be a complex concept since people shade the full truth in a variety of ways, and not all of them would be called dishonest. In the practice of leadership, however, the concept of honesty is simple; it boils down to being sincere and forthright to *everyone*. So, instead of asking yourself, "What if I tell my people the truth and they don't like it?" ask, "What if I'm not totally honest and they find out?"

* **Integrity: We act in a manner consistent with our words and beliefs.** One of the worst things a leader can do is lecture people about how important something is and then do the opposite. You can't just give lip service to your principles, morals, and values; you have to live them every day. Remember, leaders don't just preach good character; they embody it.

✳ **Respect: We treat others with care and consideration.** You want respect, and so does everyone else, so
think about what it means to you, and you'll understand
how to give it to others. At Disney World, Cast Members
are expected to show respect to everyone they come
into contact with, regardless of their skin color, religion, culture, gender, sexual orientation, or anything
else. Like all good values, respect pays off on the bottom
line. Treat people with care and consideration, and
they'll go the extra mile; treat them with *disrespect,* and
they'll undermine you at every turn.

✳ **Courage. We pursue our beliefs with strength and
perseverance.** Most organizations do not foster the
right kind of courage. On the contrary, they often make
people feel so insecure that they are afraid to speak the
truth. In fact, the failure to speak up when things aren't
right is one of the biggest problems organizations face.
Think of all the people at Enron who knew what was going on but kept quiet, or all those who clam up when
someone in their organization makes an inappropriate or
offensive comment. Having the courage to tell the truth
may not make you popular. But it pays off in respect and,
more important, in *self*-respect.

What's more, the cost of stifling courage is huge, because it puts a lid on bold new ideas and creative risks.
Remember, every single person in your organization
knows something you need to know, and some of them
might be afraid to tell you. If you make it safe for them
to tell the truth, you'll have stronger business results.

✳ **Openness. We share information freely.** By ensuring
that everyone has access to information, you send the

message that every person is important (remember Chapter Three) and that you want each and every one of them to participate. That's why Disney leaders consistently garner ideas from Cast Members that they could never come up with themselves. If you do not set an example of openness, you will not be trusted; if you're not trusted, you won't have credibility; if you don't have credibility, you will not have influence; and if you don't have influence, you'll be a leader in title only.

✳ **Diversity. We seek, value, and respect differences among our fellow Cast Members.** In Chapter Three I tell you about RAVE—respect, appreciate, and value everyone—which describes the culture of diversity at Disney World. When it comes to diversity, the real goal has to be complete and total inclusiveness, and you should settle for nothing less. I suggest you read and reread Chapter Three at regular intervals because when you get this one right, the rest of your business will function far beyond your greatest expectations.

✳ **Balance. We strive for stability and vitality in our lives.** My mother-in-law, whose name, Sunshine, matches her outlook on life, once said to me, "Lee, if you boys would take a nap every day, you would do better work." By "boys" she meant me and other high-ranking executives, and "naps" was her shorthand for rest and recreation. She was certainly right. At Disney, we believed so strongly that employees with balanced lives did the best work that we made it one of our core values. We wanted people who were happy at home, happy at work, and healthy in body and mind because that's what makes organizations strong. Create an environment in which a father can leave work to see his child in a school performance or a mother can get support in solving a day care problem, and you'll be paid back a hundredfold. If you *don't* get this right, you'll lose good people, especially parents who know what their most important leadership responsibility is. Even if they don't quit, you will lose their commitment.

Those seven Disney values have paid huge dividends in service excellence, Cast Member loyalty, and bottom line results. But I want to add one more to the list because I think it too should be one of every organization's values: **have fun.** Most of us spend more time at work than we do at home, and it shouldn't be toil and drudgery. I believe that leaders have a responsibility to use their authority and stature to make work enjoyable. If you create a culture of inclusion and enjoyment, with a strong set of values, your organization will hold together in times of trouble, and you'll laugh your way to robust profits.

3. Train for character, not just skill. It is imperative that, first and foremost, you as a leader solidify your own character and identify what you stand for. Your next task is to help everyone on your team to do the same. Remember, you're training future leaders, not worker bees, so you need not only to teach employees how to do things like use computer software and handle customer complaints but also teach them to develop the character traits and values they should bring to their jobs, such as kindness, courtesy, and reliability. The people you lead should understand that they undergo two very different but equally important types of training: (1) specific skills, and (2) what's expected of them as ethical human beings. And remember, in your training people to have good values, the most important part of the curriculum is how you, the leader, *live* the values. As Albert Einstein once said, "Setting an example is not the main means of influencing another, it is the only means." So don't just talk your values; walk them, visibly and consistently, day in and day out.

Every day at Walt Disney World I saw the impact of training for character on business success. I'll never forget, for instance, the man who had a heart attack at a Disney resort. Luckily, a frontline Cast Member in a quick-service restaurant knew exactly what to do; he immediately called 911 and then started doing CPR himself. As a result, the man was stabilized quickly and raced to the hospital. That the Cast Member knew how to save the man's life is a testament to the company's meticulous training in how to handle safety and health emergencies. But what was *really* impressive was that the same Cast Member went to the hospital later on to see how the man and his wife were doing. Not only that, but once the man was released from the hospital, that Cast Member checked on the couple every day for the rest of their visit and months later even sent them a Christmas card. That's a testament to training for character.

Here's another story about a time the Cast at Disney showed true character. At a place as big as Disney World, it's inevitable that Guests will lose things—whether a cap, an autograph book, a camera, or a cash-filled wallet. Well, on this particular occasion, at the Disneyland Resort in Anaheim, the lost item was a tooth. When a little boy's tooth fell out while he was in the park, his mother washed it off in the nearest water fountain. But she dropped it, and it slid down the drain. The child was distraught because the tooth fairy would not be visiting his pillow that night. But then, a Cast Member who had witnessed the scene called the maintenance department, and someone came and opened the drain. Still, the tooth was not to be found. So the Cast Members on the maintenance staff told the family to meet them at five at Guest Services, near the park exit. At the appointed time, they presented the tooth in a beautifully wrapped box and told the child that Tinker Bell had found it. In actuality, the maintenance team had made a fake tooth in their shop, but it looked real enough to fool the euphoric child. Needless to say, making fake teeth to please young children was not in the team's job description. But going the extra mile is what people with character do. They are fully committed, meaning they're prepared to go all the way.

As all Cast Members are told, it is not magic that makes Disney work; it is the way the Cast works that makes Disney magical. The Cast Members I just described created magic for the Guests whose lives they touched, and don't think that doesn't matter when their families plan their next vacation or recommend a destination to a friend.

4. Teach your values. Depending on their company's culture, some leaders commit their values to writing and teach them explicitly to their employees, while others communicate them mainly through example and everyday interaction. However you do it, make sure everyone in your organization knows what you stand for and is guided by the same set of principles. Here are two examples of companies, one large and one small, that were inspired by the Disney example to teach their organizations' values to their employees and build a culture around them.

After attending a Disney Institute training program, executives from Guardian Industries, the multinational manufacturer I introduced in Chapter Five, were intrigued by the notion of creating a company culture by design, rather than simply leave it to chance. Of course, like every organization, Guardian already had a culture, with certain values and norms, but it was implied, not spelled out. Employees who had been around for a while knew what the company stood for, but Guardian was growing at a rapid clip and hiring people from other companies, and the leaders were concerned about preserving the company culture. They wanted to make sure their core values would be passed along to new generations of employees and be maintained consistently throughout their global operations. After their Disney Institute experience, Guardian's top leaders hammered out a formal document that came to be called the Guardian Way, which describes the six core values the company lives by. Although the values are not posted as such in any of the company's plants or even on its Web site, they are taught by example, and their essence is communicated to every employee, beginning with the interview process for potential hires. "We can teach them how to make glass or building products, but we can't teach them character," says a Guardian executive. Still, you can model it. When leaders behave in accord with the organization's values, they get translated to the people on the ground, even if they never see a written statement of those values. As a result, Guardian has forged a vibrant, inclusive culture with a focused sense of purpose that is consistent at its worldwide plants despite vast differences in language and customs.

Another organization that was inspired to formalize its core values and teach them to its employees is America's Second Harvest of South Georgia, the small nonprofit you met in Chapter Eight. When Frank Richards, the CEO, learned at the Disney Institute that a leader's actions always tell a story about his or her values, he was inspired to spell out the values that guide his company's vision and have every current and future employee sign on to them. So with the input of the entire staff, Frank and his leadership team formulated concise statements of the company's culture, mission, vision, branding, and role, all of which everyone in the company is expected to understand and abide by. The statements are shown to every job applicant and every volunteer, so they know what's expected of them; they are posted in break rooms and printed in company handouts; and they are reinforced routinely by Frank and other leaders and referenced in staff meetings when they make decisions.

Those are two very different examples of how organizations large and small can articulate and teach their core values. Your methods may be quite different from both of theirs, and that's OK. What matters is that you look deeply into what values truly matter to you, describe them clearly, and teach them effectively to those you are called upon to lead.

At the end of your life, no one will care what titles you once held, or how much money you made, or what a big shot you thought you were. If you really care about your legacy—and you *should* if you want to be a great leader—then take a long, close look at your values and the principles on which they are based. If your character is strong, and you build your actions faithfully on that foundation, you will be remembered as a leader worthy of being followed.

Fairness, honesty, respect for others, cooperation, integrity, courage, caring: These and similar virtues are what give you moral authority, and that is the strongest and most lasting kind of authority a leader can have. When you have that moral authority, people will trust you and believe in you, and then you can accomplish anything you dream of.

ACTION STEPS

* Know what you stand for, and live by those values every minute of every day.

* Burn this fact into your brain: People will not be committed to you until they are certain you are committed to them.

* Always tell the truth; spin and manipulation create distrust.

* Be kind, sensitive, and respectful to all, even when you are coaching and counseling them on their performance. A strong leader is a tough leader, not a hardhearted one.

* Never humiliate anyone. You do not have the right to.

* Never do anything to hurt someone's self-esteem or self-confidence. No one has the right to do that.

* Display the courage to stand up for what is right in all parts of your life.

* Never do anything illegal or almost illegal, and never ask your employees to do so.

* Be open with everyone, and encourage them to be open with you.

* Create a diverse workplace, and then respect the differences in everyone around you.

* Take the time for relaxation and fun, and encourage your team to do the same.

✳ Make sure everyone you lead knows what your company's values are and teach them to follow those values themselves.

✳ Remember that your influence as a leader rests on the strength of your character and that if your character is not strong, neither will be the legacy you leave behind.

CHAPTER THIRTEEN

LEADING INTO THE FUTURE

Like it or not, you *are* a leader, whether you're the CEO of a multinational corporation, a first-time manager, or a part-time employee. You may be a great leader or a good leader, or you may still have a lot to learn, but if you've read this far, you have the heart of a leader and the potential to become an even better one than you are today. So it's very important to remember, as you go about your business and your personal life, that every choice you make matters a great deal. You have the opportunity to make a huge difference, not just to your organization's bottom line but to the lives of other human beings. As I say in Chapter One, leadership is a whole lot more than a role or title; it's a serious *responsibility.*

And that responsibility has never been greater than it is today. The world we live in—that same world in which your business operates—is more complex, unpredictable, and interconnected than ever before. As a result, your decisions and behaviors reverberate across many lives. What's more, the demands of leadership are different now than they were in the past. One reason is that the people you lead and, even more so, those you will lead in the future are better educated, better traveled, and far more plugged in to global information networks. They are also much more diverse, consisting of as many women as men and representing a vast array of races, religions, nationalities, and ethnic groups.

The generation now in their teens and twenties will enter and rise in their careers with different expectations, needs, and wants than their parents had. Not only is lifelong employment with one company no longer the norm, but young workers want flexible, nonauthoritarian environments, where they are respected as individuals and allowed to develop to their full potentials. They want meaningful work, interesting challenges, and balanced lives, and they expect to be involved and appreciated from day one on the job. They also won't tolerate the kinds of disrespectful treatment that many workers my age put up with early in our careers. They don't want to be regarded as subordinates by their so-called superiors; they want to work with humble leaders who are focused on their work rather than on their status.

They are more creative and productive as well. As I was writing this chapter, I came across an article titled "How Companies Can Encourage Innovation."* Citing experts in business and economics, the article points to creativity and innovation as the keys to competitiveness. One of those experts, Richard Florida, author of *The Rise of the Creative Class*, notes, "We're moving from an industrial economy to a creative economy," and creative people "provide a critical stimulus for economic growth." The article cites a survey showing that 88 percent of American workers consider themselves creative, but less than two-thirds of them think they're fulfilling their creative poten-

---

*Marilyn Gardner, "How Companies Can Encourage Innovation," *Christian Science Monitor*, October 15, 2007.

tials at work. Now, here's the kicker: Nearly 30 percent of those surveyed would take lower salaries to work for companies that value their creative input, and 20 percent are willing to move to different cities to work for such companies. People like that—and there are more and more of them every day—don't make employment decisions based solely on income opportunities. They base their decisions on their interests, their values, and, most important, the way they are treated in the workplace.

They're also not as obsessed with becoming the head honcho as people used to be. Many of the younger people entering the workforce grew up in homes where Mom and Dad were single-mindedly focused on their careers. They saw the consequences of an imbalanced life—not spending enough quality time with loved ones, wrenching divorces, stress-related illnesses, and so forth—and they do not plan to repeat the same mistakes. They will work hard and do a great job, but they are not willing to give up their lives for their jobs or their companies.

Bottom line: Companies whose leaders know how to attract, develop, and keep those smart, energetic, creative employees will be the winners of the future—and the future is coming fast! The times, they really are a-changin', and if you don't adapt to those changes, the people you lead will start disappearing in droves. However, if you put into practice the common sense strategies and principles outlined in this book, I can guarantee that your people will reward you with loyalty and excellence, making your business results soar.

Keep in mind, however, that organizational cultures do not change overnight. It can take time to create a completely people-centered, respectful environment. As a leader, you'll need not only a great vision and skilled implementation but also patience, persistence, and a strong will. At *Walt Disney World®* Resort, we learned that about 20 percent of the people in an organization are active change agents, another 30 percent or so resist change, and a full 50 percent have the potential to go either way, depending upon how they are led. My advice is to make that last group your primary target. Of course, you should educate and mentor all three groups, but give the fence-sitters the lion's share of your time and energy. Once you prove that you are committed to them, they will become committed to you and your organization, and this will tip them in the direction of becoming strong leaders themselves.

The fact that change takes time is no excuse to put off getting started. You need to get moving—not tomorrow, and not today, but *yesterday*. After all, time is going to fly by, so don't waste a second of it. As a leader, you have to make many tough choices, and that process starts now. And when making those tough decisions, always consider their impact on each leg of what Disney calls the three-legged stool: Guests (customers), Cast Members (employees), and business results. By clearly thinking through the effect your choices will have on these three legs, you are taking everyone's concerns into account. Once you do, go ahead and make your decision and act on it.

Above all, never make the mistake that far too many leaders make: underestimating their impact on others. Everything you say and do matters, perhaps more than you realize. Remember the wise words of my wife, Priscilla: Be careful what you say and do; they're always watching you and judging you. People will not be committed to your leadership unless they can trust you as a competent professional and respect you as a person of good character. Win their trust and earn their respect, and I guarantee you too will create magic in your organization, in your career, and in your personal life as well.

DISNEY INSTITUTE

In this book I have described the leadership principles that make Disney one of the world's best-run companies. But you can learn only so much from a book. To truly discover the business behind the magic, there is no substitute for experiencing a Disney Institute program.

Since 1986, Disney Institute's professional development programs have been attended by millions of people from virtually every industry worldwide, including more than half of the Fortune 100 and leading companies in continental Europe, Asia, Latin America, and the United Kingdom, as well as government agencies, nonprofits, and other organizations. The institute offers a comprehensive array of educational programs at several locations, including the *Walt Disney World*® Resort in Florida, the *Disneyland*® Resort in Southern California, and, increasingly, at international locales. The programs really come to life at Disney locations, where it's possible for participants to see the principles in practice. But when it's more appropriate, they can also be delivered at the organizations' locations. There are open-enrollment programs year-round, and people from a wide variety of organizations can attend; all you have to do is sign up. Custom programs can also be designed for a particular organization or industry. The Disney Institute also provides keynote speakers (I'm one of them) for conferences and other professional gatherings and conducts special workshops in various locations. Regardless of the location or program format, Disney delivers focused training on what it does best, offering such topics as Leadership Excellence, Quality Service, Loyalty, People Management, and Organizational Creativity.

Immersive, multiday open-enrollment programs are offered throughout the year to individuals and small groups. Keynote presentations, three-hour workshops, team-building programs, and other offerings can be arranged directly with Disney Institute representatives. Every program artfully blends meaningful content with Disney's renowned storytelling ability to provide a powerful development experience.

Truly distinct from other professional development training, Disney Institute programs give participants an opportunity to learn how to apply Disney's best inside practices to their own companies. Disney resorts and theme parks become living laboratories where well-trained facilitators transport you out of the classroom and into the real world, taking you behind the scenes for an up-close look at Disney's magic-making practices. Attendees invariably come to see their business issues in an entirely new light, and they return to their offices inspired and equipped to implement innovative practices. The Disney Institute offers you the unique opportunity to go both onstage and backstage and see firsthand how the Disney magic is created. I assure you, whether you're the newest member of the management team or its most seasoned executive, you will come to see your organization in an entirely new way and leave better prepared to lead it toward better business results.

For more information, phone 407–566–7625 or go to the Disney Institute Web site, www.disneyinstitute.com.

INDEX

accountability, 60, 90, 132, 239–40
America's Second Harvest, 172, 256
appreciation, 35, 188, 199
ARE (appreciation, recognition,
 encouragement), 188–207
 action steps, 206–7
 catch them doing something right,
 194–97
 for frontline employees, 202–3
 include their families, 199–201
 part of routine, 203–4
 public, 197–99
 recognize and encourage good
 ideas, 201–2
 recognize employees by name, 193–94
 spend meaningful time with
 employees, 191–93
 watch your language, 204–5
Army, U.S., 227–28
audit exchange plan, 155–56
authority, 60, 64–65
availability, 43–45
award pins, 195–96

balance, 252–53
Biggs, Terrence, 19–20
Blanchard, Ken, 50
Blee, Robert, 219
Boice, Liz, 95
Bostick, Chris, 95
brainstorming, 183
brand, importance of, 85–86
Buffett, Warren, 209, 210
bulletin boards, 136

Carter, Rilous, 241
Cast Holiday Celebration, 197–98
Cast Members, 4

core values for, 250–53
 empowerment of, 59
 Four Guest Expectations, 53, 204
 grooming standards for, 238
 Guest interactions with, 7
 involvement in hiring, 91–92
 leads, 74–75
 meaningful time with, 191–93
 overtime, 158
 promotion of, 104–6
 training of, see training
 turnover rate of, 5, 34, 35
character, 247–59
 action steps, 258–59
 and ethics, 248–50
 training for, 253–55
 and values, 250–53, 255–57
Clark, Liz, 60–61
COACH, 124–25
Cockerell, Daniel, 29, 115, 200
Cockerell, Jullian, 193–94
Cockerell, Lee:
 career of, 7–8, 19–31
 with Disney World, 4, 8, 30–31, 244
 early years of, 17–19
 entering the hospitality business, 19–21
 reputation of, 35–36
Cockerell, Priscilla Payne, 22, 23, 26,
 29, 78, 230, 242, 244–45
Collins, Jim, 243
commitment, 232–33
communication, 47–48, 125
 channels of, 68
 feedback, 136–38
 language, 204–5
 one-on-one, 136
 optimizing, 69
 in training, 133–38
competition, 218–19
confidentiality, 177–78

Conglose, Jamie, 11
Conrad Hilton Hotel, Chicago, 22–23
constructive criticism, 197
Cooperstown Dreams Park, 12
corporate culture, 51–52, 191, 255–56,
    262–63
Costco, 147–48
courage, 251
Covey, Stephen R., 212
creativity, 261–62

Dare, Bud, 98
Davis, Bud, 25
Davis, Marsha, 190–91
Disney, Walt, 6, 118, 146, 169–70, 240
Disney Institute (DI), 13–16, 31, 264–65
Disneyland Paris (Euro Disney), 7–8,
    28–29, 56–57
Disney World, see *Walt Disney World®*
    Resort
diversity, 252

Einstein, Albert, 254
Emmer, Greg, 124
encouragement, and ARE, 188
ethics, 248–50
Euro Disney, 7–8, 28–30, 56–57

Farmer, Odette, 105–6
feedback, 136–38, 153, 163
    about yourself, 182–83
    and ARE, 194–95
    brainstorming, 183
Florida, Richard, 261
Flynn, Mim, 60–61

Garcia, J. R., 90–91
Garff, Royal, 214
Gold Fields Limited, 130
Great Leader Strategies (GLS), 11, 12,
    31, 35, 208, 232
Green, Judson, 6, 7, 30, 58

Green Tabasco Award, 78–79
Guardian Industries, 92, 255–56
Guestology, 221–23
Guests:
    exceeding expectations of, 116
    Four Expectations of, 53, 204
    interactions with Cast Members, 7
    satisfaction of, 5, 7, 11, 54, 65
Guest Service Guidelines, 127–29

Hannig, Dieter, 36, 65, 85, 95, 124
Harvey's Hotel and Casino, Lake
    Tahoe, 37
Hesselbein, Frances, 205, 248
Hilton Hotel, Washington, D.C., 20–22
Hilton Inn, Tarrytown, New York, 24, 248
Holmes, Phil, 201
Holz, Karl, 65, 95, 104, 244
honesty, 250
Horoho, Patricia D., 14
humility, 243–45
humor, 240–41
Hunt, Trish, 12
hurricanes, 1, 2, 114–15, 158–59

inclusion, 34–55
    action steps, 54–55
    availability, 43–45
    communication, 47–48
    corporate culture, 51–52
    don't micromanage, 50–51
    everyone matters, 36–38
    expectations, 53–54
    forget chain of command, 49–50
    know your team, 38–39
    let your team get to know you, 39–40
    listening, 46–47
    RAVE, 35
    reach out to everyone, 41–43
    sincerity, 40–41
    stand up for the excluded, 48–49
information gathering, 208–29
    action steps, 228–29
    business fundamentals, 215–16

collect knowledge, 209–12
expand horizons, 223–26
fill in the gaps, 212–15
follow the compass, 222–23
keep up with colleagues, 219–21
keep your people ahead of the
  pack, 226–27
learn from competitors, 218–19
learn from the best, 216–18
study your customer base, 221–22
integrity, 126, 250

Janik, Stephanie, 124

Kalogridis, George, 88–89, 227
Katheder, Thomas, 59
Kelts, Marylynne, 96
Kleiser, Peter, 21–22
Kotas, Laurie, 51, 77

leadership:
  competence in, 88, 213
  DI training, 14–15
  for the future, 260–63
  importance of, 7, 8–10
  and inclusion, 34–55
  and integrity, 126
  and management, 160
  strategies of, 10–13
Lefaivre, Al, 97
Lewis, Jim, 124
listening, 46–47, 150

Magical Moments, 131–32
Main Street Diary, The, 133–34, 180, 196,
  198
management, by walking around,
  169–73
management competence, 87, 160, 213
Manent, Jeanette, 101–2
Marriott, Alice, 235–36
Marriott, Bill, 80, 139, 205, 235–36, 239

Marriott, J. Willard, 235–36
Marriott Hotels and Resorts, 223–25, 242
  Chicago, 109–10, 187
  Philadelphia, 25–27, 189, 239
  Springfield, Massachusetts, 28, 29,
    119–20, 126, 143–44, 170–71, 234
  Washington, D.C., 217–18
McDonald, Stuart, 96
McGonigle, Jim, 21
Meeks, Kevin, 52
meetings, 71–73, 135, 174–77
Mercedes Homes, 96, 123, 155
micromanagement, 50–51
Miller, Jan, 100
Miratsky, Ken, 90, 155
Mission Statement, 121–22

Nabbe, Tom, 9–10
Nanasi, Andy, 200–201
newsletter, 133–34
Norsworthy, Alice, 95

observation, 124–25
openness, 251–52
organization, 159–61
organizational structure, 57–58
  action steps, 83–84
  clear responsibilities, 63–64
  eliminate extra layers, 68–70
  eliminate overwork, 70–71
  make every position count, 65–68
  meetings, 71–73
  never really done, 80–83
  redesigning, 58–62
  resistance to change, 76–79
  responsibility/authority, 64–65
  responsibility for change, 73–75
  risks, 75–76
  winning, 79–80
O'Toole, Dennis, 23

partnership, 241–43
Payne, Charles N., 247

Pensula, Sam, 114
people, 85–113
  action steps, 112–13
  ask revealing questions, 99–100
  check candidates personally, 97–99
  clones, 88–89
  constant evaluation, 106–7
  define perfect candidate, 86–88
  demonstrate their expertise, 102
  describe job completely, 95–97
  direct reports, 174
  don't lose touch, 111–12
  find a good fit, 93–94
  find what really matters, 101–2
  hire smarter than you, 94–95
  if job doesn't fit, 107–9
  involve team in selection, 91–92
  keep ahead of the pack, 226–27
  leadership competence, 88, 213
  look in unlikely places, 89–91
  management competence, 87, 213
  nurture and promote, 104–6
  select best candidate, 103–4
  talent vs. résumé, 92–93
  technical competence, 86–87,
    212–13
  technological competence, 87–88,
    208, 211, 213
  termination, 109–10
  use structured interviews, 100
Performance Excellence, 10
Peters, Tom, 6
positive attitude, 236–38
Powell, Colin, 198
processes, 145–67
  action steps, 166–67
  ask what, not who, 147
  audit exchange plan, 155–56
  employee input into, 151–55
  fine-tuning, 146
  listen to customers, 147–48
  organization, 159–61
  periodic evaluation of, 164–65
  personal, 159–62
  resistance to change, 162–64
  speeding up, 148

  think ahead, 158–59
  time management, 160–61
  updating, 156–58
  what's working, 149–51
productivity, 69
professional contacts, 220
professionalism, 230–46
  accountability, 239–40
  action steps, 245–46
  commitment, 232–33
  full-time, 238–39
  get the job done, 233–35
  humility, 243–45
  humor, 240–41
  image, 238
  model appropriate behavior, 230–31
  partnerships, 241–43
  positive attitude, 236–38
  reputation, 231
  standards, 235–36

RAVE, 35, 252
recognition, 188, 195–96, 227
reinforcement, 194–95
reputation, 231
resistance to change, 76–79, 162–64
respect, 35, 251
responsibility, 60, 63–65, 73–75, 260–61
résumés, 92–93
reversible-irreversible test, 75–76
Rex, Brad, 89
Richards, Frank, 172, 183, 256
risks, taking, 75–76
Robinson, Don, 226
Robinson, Doreen, 234–35
Ryan, Joan, 95

safety, 177–78, 196
Scanlon, Eugene, 23, 217
September 11 attacks, 82, 184, 244
service, 143–44
standards, 235–36
stop/start/continue discussions, 153
storytelling, 137, 214

Take 5s, 131–32
Taylor, Rich, 95
team chemistry, 93–94
technical competence, 86–87, 212–13
technical updating, 156–58
technological competence, 87–88,
    208, 211, 213
think ahead, 158–59
time management, 132–33, 160–61
Towfighnia, Eddie, 187–88
training, 114–42
    action steps, 141–42
    character, 253–55
    COACH, 124–25
    communication in, 133–38
    cross-training, 60
    exceeding Guest expectations, 116
    great service, 127–31
    informal learning, 117
    Learning Centers, 117–18
    Magical Moments, Take 5s, 131–32
    managerial, 117
    and purpose, 118–23
    questions, 140–41
    role of teacher, 123–24
    self-paced, 118
    teaching by example, 125–27
    time management, 132–33
    Traditions, 116
    for unexpected, 138–39
truth, 168–86
    action steps, 186
    answer tough questions, 179–82
    confidentiality, 177–78
    for decision-making, 185
    evaluate spending, 183–85
    feedback about yourself, 182–83
    ground-level view, 173–74
    manage by walking around, 169–73
    meet with direct reports, 174–75
    small groups, 175–77
    the whole story, 178–79

Vahle, Jeff, 65, 95
value, 35

values, 250–53, 255–57
Varma, Sanjay, 28–29
visibility, 193
Volvo, 52

Waldorf-Astoria, New York, 23–24, 217
Wallace, Erin, 65, 95, 105–6, 175, 199, 244
Wal-Mart, 122, 148, 165
Walt Disney World® Resort, 4–6
    author's position in, 4, 8, 30–31, 244
    BoardWalk Inn Resort, 98
    Caribbean Beach Resort, 162–63
    Cast Members in, see Cast Members
    changing organizational structure
        in, 6, 8, 58–62
    Disney's Magical Express, 149, 211
    emergency preparedness in, 82
    Essence Statement, 121
    FASTPASS®, 148–49
    formula for success in, 7
    Great Service Fanatic cards, 199
    Guests of, see Guests
    management style in, 8
    Mission Statement, 121–22
    Partner in Excellence Award, 198
    Prize Patrols, 199
    quality service in, 5–7
    Recognize Everyday Magic, 196
    Textile Services, 32–34, 69–70, 90,
        154–55, 163–64
    transition time in, 8–10
    Vision Statement, 121
    Wilderness Lodge, 43
Weiss, Al, 7, 8, 30, 50, 58, 60, 65, 82,
    85, 101, 190, 211, 241–42
Wilkinson, Bill, 23
Wishland, 51, 77
Wolfson, Glen, 64

Yiannas, Frank, 200
You Said . . . We Listened, 201

Zais, Robin, 200

If You Want to Hear More . . .

The principles, strategies, and techniques that Lee discusses in this book are incorporated into the speeches and seminars that Lee gives around the world. Presentations are always customized to the specific organization involved, but here are some examples of his most popular talks.

Time/Life Management

Learn how to put more control into all parts of your life through this simple system for planning and carrying out your responsibilities. Lee has taught this seminar to more than 75,000 people over the past 25 years with extraordinary success.

Forget About Diversity

Diversity isn't the goal, it is the outcome of your effort when you create the working culture that Lee did during his long career with Hilton, Marriott, and Disney.

You Can Create Magic Too!

Great leaders understand what their people want the most and how to give it to them. They are rewarded with healthy organizations, excellent results, and yes, magic.

Creating Magic: 10 Common Sense Leadership Strategies from a Life at Disney

Based on Lee's book, *Creating Magic*. Available everywhere books are sold.

A Day of Learning!

Give Lee a day to present three powerful seminars to your organization's leaders and dramatically improve their abilities as Managers, Parents, Citizens, and Leaders in all parts of their lives.

Creating Magic: 10 Common Sense Leadership Strategies from a Life at Disney
It's Your Life: Time/Life Management
You Can Create Magic Too!

These seminars are based on the principles taught at the world-renowned Disney Institute.

For more information and complete contact information, please visit Lee's Web site: www.LeeCockerell.com